The Badger:

A Day to Day Account of Backpacking the Appalachian Trail

Keith Selbo

Printed in the USA

ISBN: 978-1976977367

Blaireau, Grevling, Dachs & Taxidea
Paris · Oslo · Bonn · New York

for Janis
of course

Prologue

Call me Badger[1]. I live in the foothills of the Blue Ridge Mountains. I am descended from Norwegian peasant stock.

As a boy I journeyed with my father to the ancestral farm where, from what I could make of it, the principal crop was rocks. Life there had been harsh. In the distant past, my forebears supplemented the meager yield of the soil with working vacations in Europe, returning with merchandise for which they had not paid, and servants whom they did not compensate.

Over the centuries, they increasingly came to understand the anti-social nature of their behavior, and eventually shunned it, but they left in their descendants a heritable thirst for adventure that wells up every spring like the rocks in the fields. It brought my father to America, and gave me an irresistible yearning to hike a long trail.

This is my journal.

---

[1] Badger is a trail name. It's tradition for AppalachianTrail hikers to adopt a pseudonym.

The Badger

March, 0 Miles

It's twenty after 9 PM, Sunday, March fourth, and I'm safely ensconced in my hammock after a tiring day. I had breakfast at the Hiker Hostel, and met the six hikers I'd be riding to the trail with. They were all being dropped off at the top of Springer Mountain where the Appalachian Trail begins. I had never seen Amicalola Falls so Josh the hostel owner took me there after we dropped the others off. I was the 161st through-hiker to sign the park register. My total pack weight was 32 lbs. I saw a couple in the register that were 50 lbs.!

I began walking around ten AM, and things immediately started going south. I came down with a splitting headache, and felt a little unsteady on my feet. It made the hiking arduous. It was cold and blustery all day. I was adding, and doffing layers to stay warm or avoid sweating, I made it to the top of Springer, and signed the register that's in a drawer under a rock, and then hiked down to the shelter where I had dinner with BonzeBeard before turning in.

———

The wind howled all night, and most of today. It was bitter cold, but I stayed fairly warm in my hammock. In the morning, I walked over to the shelter to cook breakfast out of the wind. BronzeBeard had suffered in his synthetic sleeping bag. A young woman named Donu had joined him when the cold drove her out of her tent.

The hiking was easy; rhododendron groves, and pine forest. Nothing is easier on the feet than a carpet of pine needles. I stopped for lunch at Long Creek Falls, which were beautiful. Weird, no one else is stopping to check out the sites. They're all bent on making miles.

I got to Hawk Mountain Shelter at 3 PM. I could have pushed on to the next shelter, but I felt it prudent to limit my miles for the first couple of weeks. This place is packed. The temperature was in the mid 30's earlier, and I saw Donu walking around in her bare feet. I'm not sure how to reconcile that with last night's tent abandonment. She told me BronzeBeard headed for town to get a new sleeping bag[1]. It's below freezing now so I'm cuddled up with my water. That means warm wash water in the morning.

—

A cold fierce wind blew across the camp all night. I didn't meet anyone in the morning who kept warm. I skipped my usual morning chores. I ate my granola, drank my coffee, and bolted from camp. In about 500 yards, there was no wind, and it was relatively warm. The shelter was located in a gap that funneled the wind. Bad siting!

The weather improved all day ending in the mid 50's with me hiking in shorts, and shirt. I ran into a hiker name of Emily *(later named Bolder)*. She said, "You're Badger, I heard about you!" I didn't ask what she'd heard thinking it was likely, "I saw this gas bag geezer, Badger, wheezing, and farting his way up Hawk Mountain."

---

[1] I never saw him again

Later Donu caught up with me when I was taking a break at Gooch Mountain shelter, and said in all seriousness, "Aren't old people supposed to be like ... slower?" I wanted to say I was only 27 but prison ages a man, but only laughed. So maybe my claim to fame is that my lifeless carcass wasn't found slumped over the rail on the staircase at Amicalola falls.

Gooch had been my goal for the day, but it was just after lunch, and there was a free shuttle to town leaving from Woody Gap at 5 PM. If I really hoofed it, I could make the six miles — I did with ten minutes to spare — and be eating pizza, taking a hot shower, and sleeping in a warm bed, which I am!

Donu left Gooch Shelter before I did but got lost on a side trail. She caught up with me about a mile before Woody Gap, and asked me if I'd split a hotel room with her. Selfless prince that I am, I agreed. With the hiker rate, it only cost us $25 apiece. She headed for Moe's for supper. I ordered in a pizza. We made our respective journal entries, completing them by hiker midnight (9 PM), and it was lights out. The shuttle back to the trail will pick us up at 7:30.

—

What I like: Hiking. There hasn't been an inch of it on this adventure so far that I haven't enjoyed. In addition, the guest book entries and encouraging emails are much appreciated. What hasn't been quite so much fun: Camping. It's been too cold. It's survivable but difficult.

What I hate: Logistics. Planning meals and re-supply. It's stressful not knowing exactly how much time it will take to cover a distance, and wondering if there will be cell coverage to call a ride. It's been getting easier as I've achieved regular success, but I can see why some people pay to have this done for them.

This morning the light banter at breakfast took a dark turn for me when Donu matter-of-factly said she was gay. She'd been telling me about her parents church, Episcopalian, and I asked if it had a part in the recent schism over gay priests. She related that their church had split off, but her parents returned to the mainstream church when she came out to them.

It was life affirming to know her parents were supportive, and I was pleased to have her confidence, but mostly I was alarmed that she'd revealed information that could compromise her safety to a virtual stranger. Off the top of my head, I knew of three women who had been murdered because of their sexuality on the Appalachian Trail no less.

I attempted to express the need for discretion while we waited for the shuttle at the Hiker Inn, but I didn't seem to make much of an impression. Possibly, I erred in not being forceful enough as I tried to instill caution without causing excessive fear[1].

The shuttle dropped us off at Woody Gap at 8:30. Donu was into the woods like a shot while I was still fussing with my gear. I passed her an hour later when she took a yoga break. Yoga breaks; who knew? After that, we leapfrogged all day.

---

[1] My concern was such that I withheld this conversation from the public version of my journal until now.

It was cold, windy, and overcast. The peaks were shrouded in mist so there were no detours for vistas this day. Everyone has been fretting about getting to Mountain Crossing because there's no camping without a bear canister in the five miles ahead of it. For us, that meant either camping just short of the restricted area, and climbing Blood Mountain the next day, or doing the ten plus miles of "difficult" terrain from Woody gap in a single day. Well, the dreaded Blood Mountain turned out to be nuthin' though I did manage to break a hiking pole on the ascent through sheer stupidity. We rolled into Mountain Crossing around 2:30.

The Crossing is a hostel, and outfitter. The hostel has a gold rush air to it. It's not too clean. The coed bunkroom is densely packed, and loud 60's music permeates the common area. The outfitter has a comprehensive inventory, and is tended by a knowledgeable staff.

I ditched my troublesome REI glomitts for a better design, and bought food for my new meal plan: sugary carbs for breakfast, and lunch, heavy fatty protein for dinner. I had been eating a big fatty lunch, and fought fatigue all afternoon.

Dinner was provided by a local church for a donation. Everyone was in the sack by 8:30 except me. I'm not tired for some reason. I picked out the last lower bunk. It was a skinny little thing that no one else wanted. Turns out it's a fold out double bed. Sweet!

—

I bolted from the hostel at 7:30 after a mediocre pancake breakfast with no coffee due to a shortage of cups. There were no views all morning owing to dense fog. It started raining around eight. Without caffeine, I couldn't get moving, and everybody passed me while I futzed with my rain gear.

It cleared up around noon. I made it to Tesnatee Gap at lunchtime. A Baptist minister was handing out junk food to through-hikers. I dove right in and quickly downed two bags of Doritos, two DingDongs, three Snicker minis, and a Coke. Donu ambled out of the woods as I wolfed down my food. She'd taken a wrong turn again, and fallen behind the pack.

The Badger and Donu

What a difference healthy eating makes. I was going over the hills like a dirt bike, passing most of the hikers who'd passed me in me morning. I made it to Low Gap Shelter at 2:30. I had more energy left but my right quad was starting to feel strained so it was a good time to stop. I used the surplus energy to shave in the hope that when it's time to hitch into the next town, I'll have a better chance of getting a ride.

All the younger hikers are eating dinner early. I'm waiting until the customary hour when the lone picnic table will be less crowded. It's in the sixties so I can sit in my hammock and type on my keyboard without a sleeping bag for a change. This crowd is the most pleasant one yet. Bolder had a trivia book. We answered questions until sundown. Life is good.

—

To all who've corresponded, thank you. To my lifelong friend Heinrich who advised me to put rocks in my pack: from playing cops, and robbers with live ammo, to teaching myself to drive when I was fourteen, you've never steered me wrong. The rocks are in. To my other lifelong friend Jane, I'm journaling on an IPhone 4 with a folding Bluetooth keyboard. Total weight approximately twelve ounces. I've been asked about pack security in hostels. All I can say is that I'm my own worst enemy. I leave things behind all the time. Things for which I have formed a deep emotional attachment like money or my IPhone are hooked to my belt loops with lanyards so they stay with me at all times. Everything else I don't worry about too much[1]. This works for me, and will continue to until the day when, inevitably, I shuffle out of the privy without my pants.

Your real enemies on the trail are bears, and mice. These vermin hold the social contract in utter contempt. They'll steal your eyeballs when you're not looking. Guard your food well.

---

[1] After all, everyone in the bunkhouse has pretty much the same stuff I do.

After dinner last night, we sat and talked in front of the campfire. When the conversation turned to hiking gear, the women turned in en masse and were soon sound asleep. Later it turned again, this time to trail towns. Uno said he met the most beautiful woman he'd ever seen in Franklin, but he'd been put off by her underarm hair to which Diva immediately responded, "Oh man, bring it!" Peals of laughter emanated from the direction of the soundly sleeping women. As it was eight thirty by then. We called it a night.

This morning I was up at six and on the trail by seven thirty. Visibility was often down to ten yards. I got cell service on a mountaintop so I posted journal entries, and read my mail. Shortly thereafter, Bolder caught up with me, and discussed arrangements for hitching into Hiawassee with Donu. It's a symbiotic relationship. They are less likely to be picked up by creeps, and I am more likely to get a ride. We agreed to camp at the site of a long gone cheese factory which would put us in striking distance of the road tomorrow. She moved on when I stopped for a snack. At lunchtime, I came across Muldoon, AT 2011, who was giving back by passing out food to hikers (trail magic in hiker parlance). I had some melon, chips, and a Coke, and it was dirt bike all over again. That Coke gives me so much quick energy I'm surprised it's still legal.

Tray Mountain Shelter is on a mountaintop. It's well below freezing, and the wind is blowing hard. I put on every stitch I own before climbing into the hammock. It's shaping up to be a difficult night.

—

More kudos: to my wife Jan, and daughter Emilie who have been getting difficult to find supplies, and replacement parts to me, and to my good friend Andy Hamm who, with his expertise in various jpeg protocol variations, has been getting my photos posted.

After a very cold night I woke up to relatively calm air. It was just below freezing but the temperature climbed all day, and by the end, I was hiking in my shorts, and T. It was about 55; perfect hiking weather.

I leapfrogged with Uno and Diva a couple of times. Today's dirt bike fuel was provided by a previous through-hiker name of Pater(?). I hope I got that right because it really hit the spot. Soft drinks would be the perfect hiking food if they only had a little more sugar.

Otherwise, the day was uneventful. I stopped a couple of hundred yards short of the trailhead to sponge off my pits, and naughty bits, and put on some deodorant for the hitch into town. It was unnecessary because the *very* hiker friendly Hiawassee Budget Inn had sent a free van out to Dick's Creek Gap that transported several of us. My replacement hiking pole was at the Inn when I arrived.

I went grocery shopping, and whom should I meet in the checkout line but Bolder and Donu. We're going to meet again tomorrow, and ride back to the trail together.

—

I entered North Carolina at 2:45 PM today. It's a day after I predicted because my guidebook doesn't include the miles of the approach trail at Amicalola

Falls. It was some of the steepest continuous climbing yet.

There are quite a few people camping around Muskrat Creek Shelter tonight, but it's an entirely new group save for Donu and Bolder. The logbook shows me gaining on people who left ahead of me. I changed my lunch regimen from cooked noodles or a Knorr Side to garlic Triscuit thins, little cheese rounds, and sixteen ounces of Tang. I chose Tang because it had fifty percent more calories than the other powdered drink mixes. I can really tell the difference in my afternoon energy level.

The crowd was up late owing to the time change, which caught me by surprise, but not my IPhone. They've just gone to bed now. It's shaping up to be another cold one.

—

It wasn't all that cold a night after all. In fact, I was too warm at times. At 5:30 AM, I dreamt it was 6:00. I awoke to mist in the hammock. Outside the fog was so thick I couldn't see the shelter not twenty yards away. I went into the woods to find my bear bag. The line it hangs from has reflector tape on it to make it easy to find in the dark, but the fog threw my headlight beam back in my face.

At some point I realized I didn't know where I was anymore, and found myself wishing I'd written something more substantive in my final journal entry when a dog barked. I knew where the dog people had pitched their tent, and was able to make my way back to the shelter. There I enlisted the help of a hiker who'd hung his bag from the same branch. I stood at the shelter with my lamp on while he walked out, and found the tree.

After breakfast, Donu said she had changed her mind about pressing on to Natahalla, and wanted to hitch into Franklin with me in two days to see a doctor about her ear. I took one look at it, and said, "You're going into Franklin today!" It was red, swollen, and had a huge blister at the top. She didn't want to go, so I rattled off the things I thought it could be, and she started to cry. I thought it might be a matter of money, and offered to lend her shuttle fare, but she said it wasn't necessary. Then Bolder offered to escort her to the Forest Service road, and call shuttle for Franklin. That settled, I hit the trail.

Bolder overtook me a couple of hours later during a break, and told me Donu had called her sister, a nurse, who said she was good to hike for the two days it would take to get to the main highway as long as the redness didn't spread,

It was pea soup and rain all day. I climbed Standing Indian Mountain, about 5500 feet, but no views were to be had. When I got to Carter Gap Shelter, the usual crowd including Donu and Bolder was already here. It was pouring so they suggested I stay in the shelter to avoid setting up my hammock in the rain. So here I am with six of my closest new friends, nestled between a woman who's through-hiking with her son, and a firefighter from Florida.

—

The rain that was falling when I reached Carter Gap Shelter continued to fall into the wee hours, and made a deafening racket on the metal roof. Meanwhile, inside the shelter someone was sawing wood at a brisk pace. Sometime well after sunset the Beagle Boys (the name I gave the group of

11

scruffy hikers who preferred not to pitch their tents in the rain) came in late, and set up shop in the crawl space under the shelter. We could hear the roar of their stoves, and much clanging of pots, and pans, and later, what sounded like an ad hoc poker game.

With the devil tap dancing in the attic, Joe's Carpentry on the mezzanine, and the Beagle Boys casino in the basement you might think I was ready to plant a fork in somebody's forehead, but fatigue builds character, and I slept right through most of it. My undoing was the hard shelter floor. I spent the last several hours sitting with my back against the wall floating in, and out of sleep.

To make matters worse, aside from me, and the mother who looked to be in her forties, everyone in the shelter had done serious time in grade school within the last decade. They can sleep twelve hours without getting up to take a leak. Not me, and making use of a P jar in such close quarters is dicey. I brought it in discretely tucked under my jacket, and stuffed it in my boot after I used it. I muffled the act with my sleeping bag, and my jacket. I couldn't hear a thing, but given that I'm half-deaf, it probably sounded like a waterfall to everyone else. Trees will have to be falling before I use a shelter again

I was on the trail early the next morning. The visibility was much improved so I took a couple of side trails to some spectacular views. Bolder was the only other hiker who took the time. Even with the stops, I moved right along. No one overtook me until I stopped to fill my water bottle, and Uno happened by. We hiked together for the rest of the day. It was all easy hiking except for a couple of sections on the way up Albert Mountain that were straight out of Snuffy Smith.

Bolder caught up with us as we stopped for lunch at the fire tower at the top of Albert, and the three of us hiked together to the shelter. We arrived around three, and enjoyed the sunny afternoon. This is the first night in my hammock that I didn't have to prepare for bed in frigid weather. Rock Gap Shelter is at the hundred-mile mark (108 for those of us who hiked the approach trail). It will be a short hike to the Highway tomorrow where I hope to catch a ride to Franklin for re-supply.

Bolder

—

It is sad that while I experience many fascinating encounters, and events daily on this hike, I can only relate a few owing to day's end exhaustion, and the fact that I am afflicted with the short-term memory of a senescent goldfish. What I remember of this day isn't very exciting I'm afraid.

I was actually sweating in my hammock last night. This morning I was again first out of the chute with most of the crowd just beginning to rise at about eight. Later this spring I'll need to fuss with my gear or something until someone else leaves because I hate clearing out the spider webs myself.

It was just a few miles to the road. Bolder the power hiker caught up with me just as I was nearing the highway. The Budget Inn free shuttle was waiting when I got there. I bid farewell to Bolder who still had two days worth of food in her pack (as well as a large library). I should say something about Ron Haven, the owner of a couple of Budget Inns as well as some other real estate from what I gather. He's also a county commissioner. He offers free shuttles for hikers to his Inns; not a selfless act to be sure, but he also helps hikers any way he can. I needed to have a spot-checked. I asked Ron where the urgent care center was, and he said he'd take me there, and back if he was around. He wasn't, but his clerk gave me the number of the local circuit rider, which diverted to take me aboard. Ron's prices are in line with or lower than his competition. He just seems like an hell of a guy. Thank you Ron.

The urgent care doctor was straight out of Seinfeld. I asked him what he thought the spot was, and he said, "I don't know *what* that is". He set up an appointment with a dermatologist/surgeon to do a biopsy the following day at 3:15. That killed any hiking plans I had for tomorrow, but it also meant I could relax for the rest of the day, which is what I was doing when the dermatologist called. He's a volunteer trail maintainer, and when he heard I was a hiker, he offered to come in early in the morning for me. All well, and good, but now I really have to scramble all over town.

Hiawassee was a village of eclectic architecture surrounded by wooded hills dotted with upscale vacation homes. The largest structure was the Baptist church. The merchants aren't shy about posting political campaign posters, which testifies to the cultural homogeneity of the place. A number of businesses such as the Ingles super market sport "American Owned" in letters as large as the name of the business itself. Franklin is much larger, and at least seems more cosmopolitan, no "American Owned" on the Ingles here. There's a river walk, museums, and an art center. I dropped my keyboard, and it broke, so far, so good with the duct tape.

—

The dermatologist took one look at the spot, and said it was nuthin'. No biopsy needed. The free shuttle wasn't leaving for an hour so I decided to hitch figuring worst case the shuttle would see me, and stop. I was getting to the outskirts of town when a trail maintainer named Dave picked me up, and drove me all the way to the trail in his Lexus.

I was late getting started. I had eleven miles to cover to get to the Wayah Bald Shelter, and thunderstorms were forecast. I made it to Swinging Lick Gap in good time. I'll leave it to the budding psych, and sociology majors out there to guess how the Gap sign was vandalized.

There was thunder all afternoon, which worried me because I'd heard the winds can be vicious on the Bald, but only a little rain fell. I put on my rain gear in time for it to stop. I walked in the rain gear long enough to dry it.

There were spectacular views from an old stone fire tower on the Bald. The mountains went to the horizon in every direction, and there was a rainbow off to the west. It was a short walk to the Wayah Shelter from the tower. The usual suspects were there already including Donu who I'll name because she told me her mother is reading this. Owing to the hour, I didn't have time to sit in on the conversation. By the time I'd gotten set up, and cooked dinner people were turning in. Now I'm watching the lightning flashes over the town of Franklin.

—

There was a thunderstorm last night. It had me jumping out of my hammock, if struggling out of my bag, pulling on my boots, and staggering can be called jumping. I lowered the tarp to keep the wind, and rain out.

I was first up and making breakfast in front of the shelter when a figure lumbered out of the inky shadows. He wore camouflage fatigues, a headlamp that he beamed right into the shelter, and had a machete slung from his belt. He looked to be about 25, and had a full beard. He resembled a thin Paul Giamatti. He said he needed to build a fire.

I said, "Fire ring's over there."

16

"Nah, I need to put it somewhere that throws back more heat like over there [against the shelter]".

I said, "That might be a little dicey what with people sleeping inside, and all."

He shrugged, settled on a spot a few feet out, and built a fire that he sat in front of cross-legged, and first warmed his hands. Then he commenced cooking. This was the semi-mythical MacheteMitch of whom I had heard but never met. He makes do with a poncho and a fleece hoody for shelter, and warmth, and a small pot for cooking. Other than that, his pack contained a small bag of food, and that piece of gear essential to minimalist hikers everywhere, an IPad. Other hikers began to gather, and I moved away as I was sure I'd pick up more of the story from others in the coming weeks. I'm a little shy around certain types. When my nephew was an intern, he attempted to give a patient some friendly advice. I don't remember what; something like "You know, I think you might get more water in that glass if you turned the hollow end up." He was rewarded with a poke in the eye.

I had a bacon cheese bagel that I cooked in a jury-rigged Dutch oven, and was on my way. Everyone else planned to push on to the Natahala Outdoor Center for one reason or another. I think I could have made it but my knees are complaining so I thought it best to give them a rest. I was taking a break at Cold Spring Shelter (a hole) when Mother and Son team overtook me, and handed me my headlamp. I'd dropped it on the privy floor that morning, and forgotten to pick it up.

Wesser Bald Shelter was deserted when I arrived so I went about futzing with my gear, shaving, and reading the pages I'd torn out of the New Yorker two weeks ago. Other people started wandering in around six. It was Zataran's Black Beans and Rice with peas for supper, and I was off to bed.

—

The day began as it typically does with me cooking breakfast in front of half a dozen slumbering hikers. After breakfast, I hit the privy, and instead of leaves for throwing on my business in the leaf bucket, there were three mice, two corpses and one still alive. Presumably, he'd murdered his compadres in their sleep.

I have no sympathy for these pack gnawing, disease spreading, food thieving minions of Satan, but starving in a bucket is far too good for the filthy creatures so I released him, wishing him a speedy, and horrible end as he scampered into the leaf litter. Next stop was the Natahala Outdoor Center, six miles away, all down hill. I made it by lunchtime. The NOC is a big complex with kayak, and raft rental, a small grocery store, an outfitter, cabins, hostel, restaurant, train station, and maybe some other stuff. I went to the restaurant where I asked for a table near an outlet for my chargers.

I got a great table right above the Natahala River. When I sat down, I could see right to the bottom. When I left an hour and a half later, the bottom was no longer visible. The river was up at least a foot. I was tempted to order the hog choker special with extra fat, but I figured if I didn't get some vegetables soon my teeth would loosen, and my hair would start falling out. Therefore, I ordered a salad, and a giant plate of ziti — that word always makes me laugh — with vegetables in marinara sauce. My batteries were still charging, and my photos were still uploading when I finished the ziti — ha ha — so I ordered coffee, and ice cream with chocolate sauce.

When I finished I picked up a care package from Jan that the outfitters were holding for me (really swell people those outfitters), and bought food. The store didn't have Tang, poon or otherwise. I was deeply disappointed. I have one serving left. I ran into Mother and Son who were planning to spend the night at NOC, and Donu, also spending the night, as I crossed the river.

I had to climb three thousand feet over six and a half miles to get to Sassafras Gap Shelter, but I felt great the whole way. I'm thinking it was the three-hour layover at the NOC giving my body a rest, and letting the tendons in my feet regain some elasticity. I plan to try a two-hour siesta next time the going gets tough.

Tonight I took a little time to patch some holes in my pack that incidentally match up with some holes wearing in me. Camping near me is JBone: a professional sky diver, and his chute-packer-wife, Tuchi, Curry: a young smoker who despite his habit, shoots up the slopes like a humming bird, and two guys I started leapfrogging with yesterday.

—

There was a thunderstorm last night. It rained heavily but no lightning came within a mile of the campsite.

Today was a good hiking day from the standpoint of distance covered, but not so hot in terms of equipment failures. My expensive Outdoor Research rain/sun hat chinstrap came undone on one side.

JBone and Tuchi happened along, and lent me a safety pin to hold it temporarily. I sewed it back in place during lunch. Someone left some trail magic on a picnic table but all that was left was a can of peanuts and a diet Dr. Pepper. To my mind, giving a diet drink to a through-hiker is like giving saccharin water to a humming bird, but I guess the diabetic hikers of which there might actually be one appreciate it. Also during lunch, the two nameless girls from Sassafras Gap Shelter showed up. They are Julia, and BabySteps taking a break from U Maryland to hike the AT. They were trying to name all the state capitols, and were stuck on W. VA. I said I thought it was Wheeling. Sorry Girls, it's Charleston.

The trail went over innumerable rockslides that were wet and slippery from the thunderstorm. It was on one of these that I slipped, and landed on one of my poles, and broke it. I've been using this brand of ultra-light pole for about 3 years without breaking a single one until this hike.

It may have been fatigue. I wanted to get to Fontana Dam as early as possible in the hope of re-supplying, doing laundry, and getting a few more miles in so I hiked for 9.5 hours. I didn't feel all that tired. I took an hour, and a half break at lunchtime to rest up, but 9.5 hours is 9.5 hours, and I was probably worn out.

Interesting crowd here tonight. Not a one save me has hung their food in a bear bag. Irony being what it is, I probably shouldn't have either. We'll see in the morning.

—

I'm stealth camped[1] well away from the shelter (called the Fontana Hilton because it has flush toilets and showers) area where a very expressive fellow was expounding loudly on the nature of just about everything. I'm not sure if I'm allowed to be here. In any case, I don't want to be because it's turned out to be near a popular parking place, and I'm not well hidden. There's a car out there with the air conditioner working overtime right now.

The day began badly enough with me losing a knee band. Vincent told me he saw it back at Cable Gap Shelter but didn't know whose it was. It was mostly down hill to Fontana Dam. I stopped along the way to pick up a temporary hiking pole. I cut it to length with my wire saw that I almost never use, and hadn't planned to bring with me. I took the shuttle from the trailhead to Fontana Village, formerly a housing complex for the Tennessee Valley Authority construction crew that built the dam, and now under fifty year lease to the Fontana Village Corporation (I think) which runs it as a resort, and a very nice one from the looks of it.

Everyone else on the shuttle got off at the grocery store. I went to the Pit Stop restaurant to stuff my face with hotdogs, cokes, and potato chips. Having thus immunized myself against overbuying, I bought groceries. Again with the no Tang. I made a feeble attempt at concocting a substitute but wasn't sure how much sugar I needed so I asked a fellow hiker name of DOS how many cups per pound of sugar. She told me I needed to buy some electrolyte replacement instead of Kool-Aid. I said I just wanted a sugar delivery system, and she looked at

---

[1] Unauthorized campsite

me as if I'd just spit in the lettuce. When I saw her this evening she wouldn't make eye contact.

At suppertime, I treated myself to a fancy dinner at the lodge. Mother and Son were there. They stopped by my table, and told me they're staying here another day.

I carefully trimmed the fat off my steak, ate it with my potatoes, then the meat, and followed that with a piece of cheesecake. I'm trying to gain a couple of pounds. As far as I can tell my weight hasn't changed, but my pack adjustments are now at their limits, and it's starting to hurt me. I don't wish to buy another pack.

It took forever to get the check because a contingent of the Illinois Outlaws was keeping the waitress busy. No complaints from me. The horn just went off in the air conditioner car. No idea what's going on in there.

—

Hikers passed my hammock, and gawked at my hanging bear bag all night. Somebody in an SUV stopped with his lights right on my hammock, got out, and shined a flashlight at me. I think it was a ranger but nothing was said, and he went away.

As I packed my hammock, Diva came around the corner having just hiked from Cable Gap in the wee hours. After that, I was making breakfast at some picnic tables. At the other end of the row, there were two people on a tabletop in sleeping bags. Eventually one of them got up, and came over to me. It was Bolder. I was sure she was days ahead now, but she'd met up with her brother, and camped with him for a couple of days. We had a nice chat before she hiked out.

Today marked my first day in the Great Smoky Mountains National Park (GSMNP). I started out with ScrewLoose, but he soon outdistanced me. It was a long uphill slog all day. I stopped at an abandoned fire tower a tenth of a mile off the trail, and 150 feet up for lunch. Smiley came up too, but only because he missed a turn, and thought he was still on the AT. I spent about an hour there. The weather was perfect.

ScrewLoose

In the afternoon thunder began to echo across the valleys. It started raining with thunder, and lightning. Lightning was striking less than a thousand feet away. I didn't see that there was much I could do about it, so I decided to present a moving target to whatever gods were assigned to my torment. I made it to Mollies Ridge Shelter during a lull. Hikers are required to stay in shelters in the park (joy of joys). This one is huge. Tarps close the front, and there is even a fireplace. No one was in the mood to start a fire though. I cooked under the outside overhang, exchanging recipes with Mo as we cooked and ate. Then I set up shop on the upper level. I was perusing the shelter logbook, and the storm was again raging when the tarp was thrown aside, and a rain soaked figure swept into the shelter exclaiming, "I Made it!" It was Donu.

—

Donu had been racing for the last two days to make up for taking the day off at the NOC, hiking long days, and camping alone in the woods with nothing but a fire for company. On the afternoon of the storm, for reasons I'm not quite clear about, she opted not to wear her rain gear. As the cold rain fell, and the wind blew, she sensed hypothermia leaking in, and moved fast, making an unheard of three miles an hour! She felt explosive relief when she reached the shelter.

The wind that was blowing when she arrived continued to roar all night. The fluttering of the tarp sounded like someone fidgeting with their gear, but that was a minor irritant compared with my back pain from sleeping on a hard floor. I doubled my pad over but thin as it is, I might as well have added an extra sheet of plywood.

This morning Donu slept in as usual while I, with no hammock to fold, was out of the chute at 7:30.

Soon I was weaving my way back and forth across the NC-TN border. I was finishing my lunch on Rocky Top, Tennessee when Donu passed by. I eventually caught up with her when she was topping off her water, and we hiked together to

Derrick Knob Shelter. We arrived well before suppertime so the afternoon was whiled away with the myriad tasks with which hikers are saddled.

I figured that I needed to hike 13.5 miles tomorrow, and another 4.5 the next day, and be at Newfound Gap at 8:15 AM to catch the shuttle to Cherokee NC. It's going to be a hectic two days.

—

I was out even earlier this morning, about 7:15. I began the long climb to Clingmans Dome. At 6340', it's the highest point on the AT. They talk about "trail legs" but in my case, it's all about trail feet, and today, I had them. The miles slid by but the pain never came. Trail conditions were optimum. There were none of the ankle twisting, pole breaking traps that have punctuated my journey previously. A couple of miles before I reached the dome, I encountered a search crew that was looking for a day hiker who'd been missing for six days. There wasn't much I could tell them. I arrived at the Dome earlier than expected. It was misty so I didn't bother to climb the observation tower.

I reached the turn-off to the shelter Donu and I planned to stage at for our run to New Found Gap at 3:30. I weighed sleeping on the hard floor against the Cherokee Microtel. Donu was committed to going into Gatlinburg, and me to Cherokee so it was an easy choice. I was off. It was mostly down hill. I've perfected a technique for vaulting down slopes, and steps on my poles. It works well in the absence of obstacles of which there were few. Under optimum conditions, I can get more than six feet in a single stride. I flew down the slopes. I achieved a personal best of 18 miles in a single day, and an average speed of over 1.8 miles per hour.

At New Found Gap, the lot was full of trucks, and police cars that were engaged in the search for the missing hiker. I met the man's father, and told him of my encounter with the search crew several miles to the Southwest. A few years ago, a blind hiker was lost for about as long in Virginia, and was found in good health. I hope for the same outcome here.

Shortly thereafter, I was approached by a man who said he'd give me a ride to Cherokee. We talked as we drove. He proved to be genial, and well informed. His name is Pat Brennan. He's retired from the Toronto Star but still roams the continent writing travel articles for the paper. He drove all over Cherokee to get me to the Microtel, but refused any form of compensation.

I registered at the Hotel then went to the Chinese all you can eat buffet. I ate all I could. When I paid my bill, they said they didn't want to see me again.

—

They didn't actually tell me not to come back; they just looked like that's what they wanted to say. I forgot to mention a man handing out goodies at New Found Gap. He attempted to hike the AT a couple of times but was thwarted first by Lyme, and then by MRSA, and he had a divot in his foot to prove it. It was sobering to be reminded that the will to hike may not be sufficient for success.

I had a big breakfast at the Waffle House, and shopped for supplies at the Food Lion. TANG!!! Then I headed for the Post Office to pick up my summer gear, and new hiking pole. Jan included some cheesy mashed potatoes that I fixed tonight. They were delicious when liberally doused with Parkay Squeeze.

I took a bus to the edge of town, a ride that took me past the innumerable kitsch malls that grew up without the fuss, and bother of planning, or zoning, and occupy virtually every flat spot in town save for the space occupied by one of the few multi-story buildings; the casino. The casino complex dwarfs all other structures in the community.

My stop was at the GSMNP Visitor Center where I began hitching. It was about an hour before a forest ranger gave me a lift back to New Found Gap. It was pouring so hard when he dropped me off that my pants got soaked in the 100 yards or so I had to run to get to the restroom. I put on my rain gear, and hiked. It was slow going. The trail was often a river. I stopped at Iceberg Springs Shelter for lunch. It was only about two thirty but the people there were already getting into their sleeping bags to wait out the storm. My rain attire was warm and comfortable so I had no qualms about reentering the weather. Much of the afternoon's hike was along a knife edged ridge barely wider than the trail. I was almost to Peck's Corner Shelter when a piece of trail gave way under my foot, and I fell, and broke another pole. I think that's going to be it for the lightweight carbon poles on this trip.

I didn't get to the shelter until after eight because of my late start. I got the last slot. There were no familiar faces at Iceberg and none here either. I'm sitting outside in the dark writing this so as not to disturb anyone, but I can still hear the logs being sawed inside. Oh happy day!

—

Well, it just gets better, and better. I made a wrong turn out of the shelter in the fog this morning, and went 2 miles down a side trail turning

27

my 12.9-mile hike into 16.9 miles. The clouds rarely parted. It was cold and damp most of the day. I've been hiking in some sort of conifer forest. It can be nice. The wind doesn't penetrate it the way it does the dormant deciduous forests I've been traversing, and the floor is covered with beautiful green moss, but on days like today with no sun, it's dismal. I feel like I'm hiking the trail of doom.

Sometime during my walk, I dropped a little plastic bag that I'd put some money in just in case I lost my wallet. When I got to Cosby Knob Shelter, I broke my spoon. I managed by holding what was left of it with a miniature pliers. Once again, I don't know anyone here. They're all young men, and either they didn't notice the sign on the wall that says cooking in the shelter attracts bears, and mice or they don't care. Half of them smoke, but since there's a fire in the fireplace, it's not that noticeable. I wouldn't say they're intentionally rude — they're polite, deferential even — just not aware of the rules. This was the first of many encounters with the JerseyBoys whose company I came to enjoy.

—

It was a stormy night; dark too. We only got rain but I hear that some places got hail and snow. A couple, WalkSoftly and MakeTime2, came in while I was fixing breakfast. They'd been thrown out of the last shelter because hikers with reservations showed up. It's complicated. Read the shelter regulations for GSMNP online if you want to know how it works.

It was 35 in the shelter when I got up. I had stayed comfortable in my summer bag by wearing most of the clothes and rain gear I have with me.

My only difficulty was the discovery at breakfast that at 35 degrees, honey flows like cold steel. I was a little late getting started likely due to residual depression over yesterday's events. The rain was followed by cold, blowing mist.

I arrived at Standing Bear Farm Hostel in mid-afternoon. It's a crazy place. There is no office. The owner, Curtis and his two assistants stand in the yard or sit by a fire dispensing information. You put your trail name on an envelope and write your charges, food, laundry, room etc. as they are incurred. When you leave, you fill the envelope with the cash you owe, and drop it in a slot in the hostel store.

For accommodations, the choices are bunkhouse ($15) or the cabin ($20). The cabin is palatial. It has two double beds, a loft, a space heater, lamps, a desk, and lots of outlets for charging electrics. I was the only one to take the cabin, but later ScrewLoose showed up. I showed him around, and knowing a good deal when he saw one, he took the other double bed. Our boots are drying in front of the heater. Everyone else is jockeying for boot space around the fire in the yard. ScrewLoose zeroed in Gatlinburg with Smiley which is how we ended up here the same day. He said he saw Donu there touring with Avatar. They all shuttled back to the trail together. He thinks they're a shelter or two behind us.

I fixed myself a big dinner. I had a deep-dish pepperoni pizza, two cokes, a root beer, a V8, a cheese Danish, and an ice cream bar. I asked Curtis if I could buy a spoon to replace my broken utensil, and he gave me one for nothing. I went to the shower and weighed myself. I'm down eight pounds from when I started. I'm not sure what to do about that. Even out on the trail I frequently stuff myself until I can't look at food. I snack several times between meals, but I can't seem to put away the 5000 or so calories needed to sustain eight hours of hiking. I know. We should all have problems like this.

No phone service here. There was service where the trail crosses I40 but I didn't realize it until it was a mile behind me. I suppose I could have gone back and done some posting but the long distance hiker has this little quirk. If you put a cocked pistol to his head and tell him to go back a hundred yards to pick up that chewing gum wrapper that fell out of his pocket, there's a good chance he'll opt for the bullet. I'll have to wait for Hot Springs, NC to post.

—

I slept in until seven AM. What can I say? The room was warm, and the bed was comfortable. I'd done little to prepare for departure the night before so by the time breakfast was finished, food bought, pack packed it was nine thirty.

The JerseyBoys passed me around ten while I was snacking on Chex Party Mix. After a previous bad experience I had made sure that I bought "original recipe" but I noticed as I was eating that this mix had sixty percent fewer calories than potato chips. You'd think that this would be a deficiency that they could easily correct with extra butter or something, but they chose simply to note the fact.

I ate lunch in the shadow of an FAA navigation beacon on Snowbird Mountain. When I was an active pilot, these beacons were the mainstay of instrument navigation. With the soon to be implemented GPS based system, they'll be an anachronism. I was called into the woods on some urgent business. When I returned, Smiley, and ScrewLoose had arrived. We discussed possible campsites. Smiley, who'd come the furthest was inclined to stay at a camping area about ten miles from the hostel. ScrewLoose thought a night under the stars on Max Patch would be nice, and I wanted to go all the way to Roaring Fork to put me within striking distance of Hot Springs. They ended up at the camping area with several other hikers I've met but whose names escape me except for Avatar. I asked him about Donu. They shuttled out of Gatlinburg together but she had a new pack, and had also overbought on food, and fell behind; probably by a day or so. I forged on to the top of Max Patch where I ate a meal of Fettuccini Alfredo and a big helping of mashed potatoes before hiking down to Roaring Fork shelter to spend the night. I'm back in my hammock now that I'm out of the Smokies.

—

To all who've written, thank you so much. I can't make individual replies but I'm deeply touched by your compliments, and words of encouragement. To those of my fellow hikers whose names I've forgotten, I apologize. Believe me, it's me, not you. Thanks for your understanding, and willingness to repeat yourselves without taking offense.

This 18-mile day wasn't at all like the first one. It was painful, exhausting, and absent of triumphal views like the one from Max Patch from which I could see virtually the entire day's hike in panorama. It was one of those stupid gestures for which we jackasses are so well known. Simply said, it was a big push to get restaurant food.

I arrived a couple of hours after the JerseyBoys I've been dogging since Cosby Knob. There's no Wi-Fi at the Laughing Heart Hostel so I headed for the vaunted Smoky Mountain Diner which turned out not to have Wi-Fi either. They're famous for their hiker breakfast buffet so I promised I'd return in the morning and do my best to put them out of business. I finally landed at the Spring Creek Tavern. It had a crowded veranda overlooking the creek, and a deserted bar where the only table with an outlet was to be found. I drank cokes as fast as they could fill my glass and ate a couple of giant cheeseburgers and a king size basket of fries. It was enjoyable fare despite its making my arteries sore. I may need to fly home for a big plate of broccoli in garlic sauce over rice before I forget what vegetables are like. I know this diet can't possibly be doing me any good, but I'm not sure what to do about it. The only guy I see getting near the necessary calories is ScrewLoose, but he's a tank. With those broad shoulders, and fireplug calves, he could carry a grocery store.

Hot Springs is the first trail town for North bounders that is situated right on the trail. It's an innovation I wish was repeated more often. Moreover, it's tiny; six hundred thirty seven people and compact. Everything is in easy walking distance. I hope to order a medium size harness for my pack from the outfitter here to be shipped somewhere up the trail, and buy food and fuel in the morning. If my package from sweet, patient Jan arrives on schedule, I hope to be at a campsite a few miles from town by suppertime.

—

I didn't get the buffet. I'm not sure they still have one. I ordered two eggs, bacon, a bowl of stewed apples, a muffin, and four pieces of French toast. I didn't so much see it as eating as stoking a boiler. It's not the hiker experience I'd anticipated.

The package from Jan was at the post office; poles, titanium Spork, and fruit treats. I went to the outfitter who fitted me for a new pack because it turns out the harness can't be changed out, and was all around very helpful. The new pack is a medium, and fits snugly high on my back with plenty of room for adjustment. When he learned I'd sent my winter gear home he was alarmed. He assured me that this time of year I'd encounter seriously cold weather on the mountains ahead. He admonished me to have my winter gear sent back, and threw a space blanket in with my new pack free of charge.

This town is great. Granite AT blazes outlined with brass are set into the sidewalk that runs down the main street. All the businesses I needed to hit are within a few yards of each other. I was passing the outfitters again after doing my laundry, and he popped out the door, and told me someone wanted to buy my old pack. I got fifty dollars for it plus the outfitter refunded what he'd charged me to ship it home. Sweet!

I checked out of the Hostel, and went to the diner for lunch. The menu listed broccoli bits among the vegetables. Bits. Small pieces, maybe just the florets I thought. I ordered some sort of fried chicken with the word honey in it, and Broccoli Bits. When my order arrived I didn't see any broccoli, and told the waitress there'd been a mistake. She pointed to what looked like Chicken McNuggets, and said, "That's them thar." I cut into one, and gooey green-flecked cheese oozed out. I know. I should have asked.

When I'd eaten all I could, I had the rest wrapped for dinner, and headed for the grocery store. I didn't want much at that point. Some crackers, and maybe a couple of celery sticks seemed like enough for six days, but I'd resolved to buy more calories, and buy I did. My pack weighed 37 lb when walked out of town. I haven't carried that much on my back since infantry training back in the sixties.

The hike out was tough. Lunch sat in my stomach like wet cement. I felt groggy, and had the feeling that a food disaster from one end or the other was imminent. Climbing the bluff above the French Broad — ha ha — River was terrifying. The trail was steep and the drop deadly. I felt unstable. As I neared the top, I had to stop looking down.

Once I topped the bluff, it was an easy walk to this pond campsite. I'd hoped that other re-suppliers leaving town late would stop here. No such luck. I'm camping alone; not for the first time in my life but for the first time on this trip, and I'm not too keen about it. Everything sounds like a bear when I camp alone. The wind rustling the leaves sounds like a bear walking in the leaves. The wind lifting my tarp sounds like a bear opening a meat locker.

—

I slept comfortably, and late. In the morning, I could hear hikers moving up the trail on the other side of the pond. Back on the trail, I was overtaken by WalkSoftly, and MakeTime, a couple roughly my age who had stayed in Hot Springs the night before. We hiked, and ate lunch together before parting ways. They continued down the trail while I broke out my New Yorker for a relaxing read.

The signature event of the day occurred after Avatar overtook me in the afternoon. We'd been hiking together for a while when we came upon a sign announcing "Trail Magic" at the home of John, and Jody Nelson, AT hikers in 1999. We went to their house, and along with a number of other hikers including another Badger, who'd been hurrying up the trail to meet the other guy named Badger, were treated to a really decent home cooked meal culminating in our choice of several desserts. I chose a banana split. I think I was a teenager the last time I had one. The Nelson's have been doing this for years. They've served over 2800 hikers. It was a great morale booster despite now having to carry the dinner they displaced up the trail to Erwin.

After supper, John passed around some Christian books that we were free to keep, but I'm pretty well set in that department. There were handshakes, and thanks for having us in their beautiful home, and we were once again on our way.

Avatar outdistanced me pretty quickly, and I hiked alone up to Little Laurel Springs Shelter. Somewhere in the last three miles, I went lame. Whatever muscle flexes the ankle to move the ball of the foot toward the shin will only do that with a lot of pain now. By walking slowly, and concentrating, I could keep the joint immobilized but at that speed, I'll be out of food long before I reach Erwin. If it's still bad tomorrow, I'll try to immobilize the joint with an ace bandage, and duct tape. I'm not sure how exactly to do that or if it will help. Perhaps you could look at the next journal entry, and let me know how this turns out.

—

Today was something of an ordeal. It started easily enough after I threw an ace bandage on my foot to help lift the ball when I walked. First came a thousand foot climb from the shelter on a good path. It was slow going, but not difficult. The trail deteriorated at the top, which aggravated my leg. To minimize the pain I tried to keep from lifting the ball of my foot. That led to catching my toe on various roots, and rocks that in turn sent fire shooting up my leg. I would then find it necessary to swear at the offending obstacle, and kick it with my good foot, and sometimes stab it with my hiking poles for good measure.

This all made for slow going. When I stopped for lunch at Whiterock Cliff, I'd only covered three miles. I was halfway through lunch when CandyMan showed up. He's a Swiss guy I met at Fontana Village. He hands out candy, mostly Swiss chocolate. I thought he was long gone, but he took a couple of days off from hiking in Hot Springs. As with others, I've been the tortoise to his hare. We had a nice chat over lunch. I asked him if he'd tried American chocolate. He said, "Yes, and it was horrible. It tastes smoky!" News to me!

Then we both were off. My leg had started feeling better, partly I'm sure due to some Aleve I took at lunch, but I soon came to the rockiest, twistiest, rock face climbingest ridge trail yet. I slowed to a crawl, and still continually aggravated the leg. I did get my first view of the Tennessee lowlands to the west, and shortly thereafter, a fire on the mountainside ahead. "Oh, very nice!" I thought.

When I reached the fire zone there was a sign that said it was a controlled burn. It reached the trail in some places, but the flames were low, and far between. I caught up with Candyman around five at Jerry Cabin Shelter. TrailMix and a prosecutor from Huntsville, AL were also there. The latter was getting off the trail, and unloading food. She gave me some decent Tex-Mex trail mix. I cooked my dinner there, but needed to move on to Flint Mountain Shelter to stay on schedule.

Trail conditions were much better, and my leg felt better but still ached, and slowed me down. I noticed a fair number of Christian books abandoned in shelters, and a couple in a tree stump. It would seem that some hikers were uncomfortable turning down the offer of the books in the face of the Nelson's generous hospitality. I got here around 9:30. I put my hand over my headlight, and let a sliver of light escape into the shelter. There in the dark lay eight silent mummies. I found a hang in a rhododendron grove nearby. Then I began wandering around in a search for bear cables or a decent limb from which to hang my food bag. I came to a tent with a light on, and asked about cables. Avatar's voice came back with the answer.

It's been raining on, and off since about four, and it's raining now. Twelve hours to go 12.7 miles. That's a new record for me. The next couple of days are shorter. If I can hold out until Erwin, I can afford to take some time off until my leg feels better.

—

Another day of limping along. It was a short hike, and my leg felt a little better but the ache and some pain going down hill kept me to about one mile per hour again. It was nice to arrive at Hogback Ridge Shelter with some time to get some chores like back flushing my water filter, and clipping my nails out of the way.

I also hope the additional down time will help with the leg. Nursing it along has sucked all the joy out of hiking, and reduced my life to counting the miles, and the minutes to my goal for the day.

There are two Boy Scouts here working on their backpacking merit badge under the supervision of four adults. The adults are using their outside voices.

My IPhone has never needed the backup battery so I've been using it to keep my little radio charged. I listened to A Prairie Home Companion tonight. I will now open my New Yorker, and read myself to sleep.

April, 334 Miles

Things got off to a good start with my leg. There was still some pain when I stumbled, but nothing like before; certainly not enough to warrant exacting revenge on the offending obstacle. I was making decent time, and as I passed under I-26, I encountered CrankDaddy, AT 2011, passing out sodas, beer, and snacks.

Lunch was only an hour off so I exercised some restraint, downing only two cokes, some moon pies, and two bags of chips. CrankDaddy told me he'd left a cooler of treats in the woods yesterday, and somebody stole it all. There's a faction hereabouts that was forced off land that the trail now traverses, and it doesn't take kindly to anyone who supports the AT. They shot up a hostel a few years back, putting it out of commission for a season. There was one bar of cell service, and Edge data. Not good enough to post to the internet, but adequate for email. I took care of some correspondence, thanked CrankDaddy, and headed on up the hill where I ran into a day hiker who said there was more trail magic at Street Gap. I increased my speed, and didn't bother to stop at lunchtime.

Sure enough, when I arrived at the gap Yonder and Janet (AT 2007) were there with a fantastic setup. Yonder was cutting a pepperoni pizza. He said it had come out of the oven 15 minutes ago, but he'd be happy to bake me a fresh one. Truth be known, he could have pulled it out of a trashcan, and I'd have eaten it. The thought occurred to me that I could ask for a fresh one, and nibble my way through this one while I waited. You know, just to be polite, but I was a little off my feed owing to the previous trail magic already in my stomach so I just said, "You've got to be kidding!", and showed them my vanishing pizza trick. I had a little room left when I was finished so I had a couple of hot dogs with all the fixings, a root beer, a banana, a bag of chips with picante sauce, and took an orange for later all the while enjoying their good company. They began closing up as I was leaving because I'd told them there were only two North bounders at Hogback, and the other had already passed by. They said the food wouldn't go to waste — they have kids at home — but I felt a little bad that others wouldn't experience their good will and generosity that day. Worse yet, I forgot to take their picture. Thank you so much Yonder, Janet, and CrankDaddy.

With my spirits buoyed, and despite a full, ok distended, stomach, I made great time. The sun came out from time to time, and each time the warmth coaxed a burst of perfume from the windflowers that cover some hilltops like snow. Before I knew it, I was overing Bald Mountain. The wind picked up, and rain started falling so I put on my cape in the shelter of a small cut. As expected, the rain immediately stopped. In no time, I was at Bald Mountain Shelter. I was eating a sandwich I'd planned to have for lunch when the sky opened up. As I ate, one hiker after another walked up, all but one of them soaked to the skin and shivering. Apparently, there is reticence in some circles when it comes to donning rain gear. The rain has stopped now, and I'm in my hammock having made much better mileage than the last two days, and holding out high hopes for tomorrow.

The wind raged all night making for fitful sleep. Calm air didn't arrive until mid morning. Today was an uneventful day. I neglected to mention that yesterday I surpassed my old record for distance hiked without re-supply. When I reach Erwin, I think it will be about sixty-seven miles.

Around noon, I found another CrankDaddy cooler. I had a couple of soft drinks, a Moon Pie, and a cookie. After lunch, I ran into CrankDaddy himself out day hiking, and thanked him. This afternoon my leg went south again, but felt fine as soon as I stopped hiking. Shortly after I reached No Business Knob Shelter, the afternoon thunderstorm hit, dumping hail as well as rain. I didn't know anyone at the shelter but as usual, it was a genial bunch. One section hiker built a bonfire that we used to dry out our gear. It's almost always a section hiker building the fire now. The through-hikers devote most of their efforts to eating, and sleeping. An ember hit my pants, and burned a small hole in the leg near a pocket. The nylon fused around the hole, so I'm just going to live with it.

I spent the evening preparing for my triumphal march into Erwin, TN tomorrow. I sponged myself off with eucalyptus soap, cleaned my fingernails, and put on my town underpants. In the morning, I'll complete the transformation with a shave, and some deodorant. It's quiet now. I can hear a locomotive climbing a grade in the distance, and a whippoorwill calling nearby.

—

I made it to Uncle Johnny's Hostel just in time for the shuttle to an all you can eat pizza place in town. I mentioned that I wanted to get a haircut

41

while I was in town so the driver, Sarge, dropped me off at Ricky Wilson's Barber Shop with directions back to the Pizza restaurant. Ricky's wouldn't have been out of place in Mayberry. I felt as if I'd been transported in time. There were several people ahead of me, and by the time Ricky finished with me, lunch was over. The shuttle made a stop at the post office where I picked up a package from Jan, and it was back to the hostel where I plan to spend the next two nights in the hope that the pain in my leg will go away for good.

When I got back to the hostel, I walked a quarter mile to get phone reception and called Osprey, the manufacturer of my pack. The basic fit has been better, but part of the frame has been irritating my shoulder blade. They gave me some suggestions. I'm not hopeful, but I'll give them a try.

The hostel is a pleasant place, situated across the road from a river. It consists of a store, a bunkhouse, a bathhouse, and a cluster of small cabins for twenty-five bucks a night, one of which I'm staying in. Hikers can tent on the lawn surrounding the cabins for eight dollars. There are several tents on the lawn tonight.

We were transported to a mall where there were several restaurant options for dinner. I chose Mexican since I hadn't yet had any on this trip, and it was the only one that served beer (hard stuff by the drink is not legal), but once the chips, and salsa were gone, so was my appetite. I don't understand why, but lately when I'm on the trail, and somebody shows up with town food, I seem to be able to eat a lot, and enjoy it; once in town, not so much.

MakeTime, and WalkSoftly are staying here while WalkSoftly recovers from an inflamed ankle. They're going to try to get a recommendation for a good breakfast place, and invited me to go with them tomorrow. Meanwhile, I'm planning for about 26 miles for the next leg. Sixty-seven was a bit much.

WalkSoftly and MakeTime

—

I had a great breakfast of eggs, toast, sausage, hash browns, more toast and coffee — I won't say how much — at the Corner Grill with MakeTime, WalkSoftly, and Applesauce, a young man on a tight budget that's getting off the trail for a few weeks. I get a free load of laundry so I let him piggyback a few things last night. Make Time gave him his toast this morning.

Erwin, like many mountain communities, plants its buildings where it can, and that has resulted in a width of about a quarter mile, and a length of six miles. It sports an admixture of architectures, fine homes, and double wides, sometimes cheek by jowl. The major industry is a big CSX yard that forms the spine of the town supplemented by a plastic pipe company, a ball bearing plant, and several other light manufacturing endeavors. The good old boys at Ricky's said the town started out as Greasy Cove, was renamed Irwin before the residents finally settled on Erwin. No reasons were given. Sarge of the hostel, a transplanted upstate New Yorker, thinks the GOB's were blowing smoke.

Fox News blares from *every* television in the restaurants that have them. The county supervisors recently struck a blow for dog freedom by deleting a prohibition of barking dogs, and liquor by the drink is heating up as the next big controversy. For all of this, I was struck by the lack of religiosity. There is barely one church per every hundred residents in this town of fifty-five-hundred. Ricky Wilson has a sign on his wall that says "JESUS", not "Jesus Saves", simply "JESUS", a common expression of exasperation.

None of these dark undercurrents are in evidence on the veranda of Uncle Johnny's where the talk runs to "you stayin', or hikin' out today?", and "How 'bout that rain last night?" shouted over the roar of the rapids.

MakeTime, and WalkSoftly will rent a car tomorrow, and drive to MakeTime's mother's house in Waynesboro to await the healing of WalkSoftly's ankle, and I'll be hiking' out, rain or shine.

—

There was more fun on my last night at Uncle Johnny's. It came out over dinner that the two German boys, Jonas and Rolf, had never heard of

44

root beer. This inspired TickleMonster to buy two liters and a gallon of ice cream. Rolf, and Jonas as well as half a dozen Americans enjoyed root beer floats on Uncle Johnny's veranda.

I cooked myself breakfast in the morning, and was back on the trail. Shortly thereafter it rained for half an hour or so. I ran into ScrewLoose who'd taken four days off to spend time with his wife, and child. That was good. He misses them, and feels a little guilty for spending so much time away. He said he'd camp on a site along the trail tonight, and encouraged me to join him. I hadn't planned to come this far, but I'd started earlier than anticipated so I decided to give it a shot.

I found this campsite in good time, but no ScrewLoose. He must have made good time too. In the last mile or so, a storm warning came over the radio predicting high winds, and quarter size hail in a band six miles north of Erwin. I've come over twelve miles, but that's in AT miles that aren't always as the crow flies. I could see Erwin for most of the day from the Ridge I was hiking.

I decided to skip the campsite, and camp across the road, which would be in the lee of the ridge. I put up my hammock, and cooked dinner under the tarp. It stopped raining as I was preparing the hammock for sleeping. There were never high winds or hail.

—

When it wasn't raining last night, it was misting. Everything was wet or damp when I packed up this morning. Yesterday I hiked farther than I'd originally planned which put me in range of the Greasy Creek Hostel for re-supply, so I got up early, and was hiking by 6:30. I'd gone a few miles when I came across ScrewLoose who was just getting up. He missed the campsite we'd discussed. Once he realized it, he made camp in the first clear spot he found.

He decided to join me at Greasy Creek when he heard it's going to drop below freezing in the mountains. He only has a fleece bag. He caught up with me when I stopped for drinks, and snacks being handed out by Mango (AT 2006), and we hiked to Greasy Creek together.

Greasy Creek is situated at the end of a winding unpaved road that once served tobacco farms in the hollow. It's operated by Connie, an intense and harried woman who does her best to please. As with Standing Bear, the place is on the honor system, but it's cleaner, and more intimate. Connie doesn't exactly do a land office business in part due to coming up on the trail so soon after Uncle Johnny's, and partly due to her psychotic neighbor who's convinced she's running a brothel for bums. He's given to posting signs up on the trail announcing the hostel's closure due to illness or a death in the family, or leaving his lawn mower running all night next to the bunkhouse.

So Connie scrapes by giving great service with a smile to the trickle of hikers who find their way here. She drove us to the store in Buladean, then to the diner, and back here for a movie. Screw Loose chose The Dukes of Hazard which we are watching as I write. Connie made an Epsom salts bath for my foot, a cheeseburger snack, two eggs, coffee, and juice for breakfast, sold me two days worth of provisions, and a few snacks. My bill came to $32.50.

—

46

Roan Mountain is the last big mountain before Virginia. My leg felt great so I attacked it with enthusiasm. The trail was well-maintained soft loam for most of the two thousand foot climb. I ate lunch a third of the way up. Shortly thereafter, I came upon a huge dump, and a pile of toilet paper next to the trail. Nice that someone was prepared for the eventuality, but not nice that they had made no effort to conceal the result. I threw a few rocks on the mess, and was rewarded for my effort with a small drop of poop that splashed back on my glasses. I can't remember ever being so happy that I that I eschewed contact lenses for glasses. All was made good by some tissues, and a liberal dose of Purell. I must not have cleaned my glasses for quite some time because it was as if a fog had lifted when I put them back on.

The highest shelter on the AT sits at the top of Roan. I dropped in to sign the shelter log, and TickleMonster, who'd passed me on the way up, took my picture. I was descending the other side of Roan when I encountered two men in their late teens or early twenties. One stepped aside but the other, a heavyset lunk with a confederate flag for a hat stood in the middle of the trail, and asked, "Where you from?" It didn't immediately occur to me that he was being confrontational. I mistook his dullard's visage, and childish syntax for simple-mindedness (not an altogether incorrect assumption), and said, "Virginia" which elicited more questions, but it soon became clear that his chief interest was whether or not I approved of his hat. I was somewhat circumspect which he took for acceptance exclaiming, "Well, some people don't like it!" to which I replied, "I think *they* might associate it with racism". That elicited a short, angry soliloquy memorializing his ancestors who died for their cause, which I assumed but did not confirm, was to perpetuate slavery. The conversation moved on to complaints about all the Yankees who are crowding out his relatives in Florida. Naturally, I was deeply sympathetic as I edged my way around him, moving away as I talked. TickleMonster caught up with me at Carver's Gap, and reported encountering the same two guys. After some discussion, the two accompanied him off the mountain to the Gap, one in front, one behind. Creepy.

I wanted to stay here at Overmountain Shelter because it's a converted barn with room enough to hang hammocks inside. With temperatures expected to drop below freezing, I thought that might be a nice luxury. It made for a long day's hike though, and while my leg never gave me any trouble while I was walking, it aches now. I hope I didn't over do it.

—

It was a short hike from OverMountain to here with one big climb over Humpback Mountain. It's interesting how much more daunting a climb seems when you can see it in its entirety. Standing in Bradley Gap, I could see the thread of the AT winding its way to the heavens. I could see the ant-like figure of ScrewLoose, who'd passed me sometime back, about halfway up. He was so far away I had to watch for some time to discern his progress.

The wind on the ascent was fierce, and cold. At times, it blew me a few steps off the trail. After some time of putting one foot in front of the other, I crossed the summit into calm, warm weather, and made the easy descent (if you discount one annoying rockslide after another) to Mountain Harbor Hostel.

The B&B is up the hill, and by all accounts very nice. The hostel is a three story affair, the first story being a working stable, the second a kitchen, bathroom, and common area off of which a semi-private room (mine) juts, and the third is a loft with four beds. The cheap food is on the honor system. Expensive items like ice cream and pizza are sold in the big house. A stream rushes between the hostel and the B&B providing soothing white noise.

I had a pizza for dinner. ScrewLoose had two. He'd suffered through the cold night at Overmountain so he's having his winter sleeping gear overnighted to a hostel 24+ miles up the trail. He plans to hike all of it in a single day so as to avoid another night in the cold.

—

I was drinking my coffee when the unhappy ScrewLoose slipped out the door, and began his forced march to Kinkora Hostel to await his winter quilt. I remembered my six-day hike from Hot Springs to Erwin with me cursing that fear mongering inbred hillbilly who scared me into sending for my heavy winter sleeping bag. Well, I've matured since then. I've taken to calling him *The Sage, and Prescient Genius of Hot Springs Who Foresaw The Cold Snap And Spared Me Untold Suffering.*

Remember MacheteMitch? It seems that Smiley did strike up a conversation with him, and later blogged about it, saying that Mitch had a lot of smoke to blow. Well, he got wind of it — remember the IPad? — and expressed his dissatisfaction in a post to the blog comments in words that Smiley found worrisome if not disturbing. There is also an unsubstantiated rumor that the police now want to talk to MacheteMitch.

In other news, Mother and Son, aka Turtle and Taken are off the trail. Taken sustained a tibia stress fracture that will take weeks to heal. After that, they plan to plane to Maine, and hike South, so perhaps I'll encounter them again at some point.

And that brings us to today, and what a fine day it was. It was one of those perfect breezy spring days that irresistibly beckon one outside. I hiked all day in sun-dappled shade, a chunk of it along a river. I ate lunch at Jones Falls; a small falls with several fountains spouting gouts of water. The problem with the Appalachian Trail is that there are just too many Appalachian Mountains in it. We need more lazy, happy to be alive hiking days through parks, and along rivers.

Rather than stop arbitrarily at a shelter, I opted to hike until I felt like stopping which I did about the time I passed a clearing with a fire ring. I fixed Kraft Mack & Cheese for dinner, built a fire, and sewed the chinstrap back into my hat. That's the second time I've had to do that. A few weeks ago, the strap came out of the other side of my $50 hat. I used one of those little hotel sewing kits that are great to have by the way. I also sewed the button back on my pants the other day.

—

There wasn't a lot of scenery today until Laurel Falls which is just 0.7 miles from where I sit now. It was cold, windy, and mostly cloudy all day. That's good hiking weather but I missed the sun. The Laurel Fork Shelter is on a ledge cut out of a bluff above a river.

The wind seems to be letting up now, but it was devilish while I set up camp, and cooked dinner. It blew leaf debris into everything I dished up, and had my tarp flapping, and snapping the whole time. It was exasperating.

Tomorrow I will break camp early, and head for Hampton, TN for re-supply. I haven't decided to get enough for a four-day hike to Damascus, VA, or plan another re-supply. I'll see what others have to say tomorrow. I plan to buy supplies and get back on the trail. Since I won't be staying in town, getting everything recharged, and uploading my journal entries may be difficult.

—

The nine miles hiked today reflects only official AT mileage, and not the four additional miles hiked to, and around Hampton, TN for re-supply. I got up early, ate an abbreviated breakfast of Pop Tarts and hiked to the side trail to Hampton. The trail came out at the end of town opposite the end with all the services. It is always thus. First stop was the post office to pick up my package from Jan. I wasn't too surprised to find ScrewLoose there picking up the package that was supposed to arrive yesterday but didn't. Once again, we made our final goodbyes, and he shuttled back to Kinkora. The postal clerk recommended Teresa's Diner for breakfast.

The dining area of Teresa's isn't much bigger than my kitchen, and it was full save for one tiny table. As I walked to it, I was beset with questions about my hike. I noticed the empty table didn't have an outlet so I asked two of the men I'd been talking to if they'd mind switching. One said, "Sure, but only if you're a Democrat". I'd have been less surprised if he'd sprouted flowers from his ears.

Being completely apolitical myself, I just smiled, and gave them a "haw, haw" as I sat down. The next surprise came from a man holding court at a big table in the corner. He said I could eat whatever I wanted, and he'd pay for it. I scanned the menu for liquor and steak. Finding none, I ordered a couple of number one breakfasts which seemed to satisfy my benefactor.

I got to work checking messages, and email, catching snippets of conversations as I went. I've been in several places like this since starting my hike, and the clientele doesn't vary much. Same drawl, same idiom, same phenotype, but here the words were completely different. There was no talk of the nanny state, the war on Christmas or the demise of the family. Conversations were going to Steven Breyer's analysis of controversial Supreme Court decisions, Obama's chances for reelection, and nuanced analysis of health care reform. Talk about a twilight zone moment!

Next stop was the Dollar General which appears to enjoy more ubiquity than Wal-Mart in these parts for re-supply. Then I went to McDonald's for lunch, and Wi-Fi. By one o'clock, I was on the road out of town. There was an 1800 or so foot climb but the weather was cool which always makes it easier, and then a long, smooth descent to Watauga Lake Shelter where I met Instigator and Expediter, an athletic couple roughly my age who started a week later than I did. It's supposed to get into the twenties tonight, so once again, I'm snuggling up to my water filter to keep it from freezing.

—

I spent almost the entire morning climbing from Lake Watauga to Vandeventer Shelter, arriving there in time for lunch. The shelter is perched on a cliff above the lake, and the view was fantastic. I perched on an outcropping, and ate as I enjoyed the view.

After lunch, I hiked along a ridge in pretty much ideal conditions and got to Iron Mountain Shelter around 4:30, which gave me more time than usual to set up camp. After dinner, I built a small fire for the purpose of getting rid of my combustible trash. As I did, more hikers began drifting into camp, and the fire acted like a magnet pulling them in. I'd never met any of them before. They were young, unafraid of plunking themselves down in the dirt or eating strange food, the strangest being Ramen with peanut butter. I enjoyed their company, but the cold drove me to bed. They're still going strong about twenty feet away. It's going below freezing again tonight if it hasn't already. I brought two hand warmers to bed with me to supplement my body heat.

I got an email from MakeTime. They plan to resume their hike where they left off in Erwin as soon as WalkSoftly is sufficiently recovered.

—

When I got out my breakfast food this morning, I dumped about a quarter cup of coffee mix on the ground. I assumed I'd neglected to zip the bag shut so I zipped it the other way, and it was still open! Thank you Hefty click bags!

At my first break, I was resting in a puddle of sunlight next to a stream enjoying a Tang stupor when DigIt (nee Diva) materialized out of the sun. I hadn't seen him since he rounded that bush back at Fontana. Shortly thereafter, Uno showed up. For two guys who differ so sharply, at least in their opinion of female underarm hair, they seem to get on well, and are seen hiking together often as not.

They started at Vandeventer, and planned to do 30 miles to make it to Damascus, VA tonight. Normally I'll hike all day, and see one or two people, but as I close on Damascus, hikers I haven't seen for weeks, and a ton I've never seen before seem to be falling out of the trees. They're all shooting for the big miles to get into Damascus at the earliest possible moment.

Damascus lists itself as the trail friendliest town on the AT (we'll see) but it's going to be there tomorrow, and probably next week, so I don't know what the pull is. I'm ten miles away, so I'll arrive there after lunch, and I plan to stay for a shower, laundry, and a restaurant meal.

There are six other hikers here at Abingdon Gap shelter who either resisted the attraction of Damascus, or just couldn't go any further. There's a pretty girl, a young German, and four veterans; two back from Iraq, and two Marine Officers using up their leave before they get out. The Marines are also raising money for wounded vets in various venues as they go, so they have a schedule to meet.

We had a good time shooting the breeze around a bonfire. Everyone else is still there, but I'm in the hammock so I can get up early, and get to Damascus before someone makes off with it.

Uno and Diva

—

Aided by benign trail conditions, I made 2+ miles per hour, and was in Damascus just after noon. The first thing I need to say is that I've seen none of the civil strife, and turmoil in Damascus that I've been reading about in the New York Times. It's been a pleasant day with many milestones, and unexpected turns. I made a complete wardrobe change-out, which is to say, I bought a new long sleeve shirt, and pants. My old wool shirt grew a crop of holes almost overnight (moths maybe?), and my ultra-light convertible pants suffered from workmanship problems and a few burn holes. I'd sewn the button back on once, but I figured when the cargo pocket began to separate from the leg, it was only a matter of time before another seam would open, so I got a slightly heavier pair of pants in the hope that I would have one less thing to worry about. Now that I think about it, I now have nothing to worry about.

After my stint at the outfitters, things just kept going my way. I was walking up to the Laundromat grumbling about having to pay 4 or 5 bucks to wash a T-shirt, my trail underpants, and a pair of socks when I ran into GoodDeeds who had a big sack full of clothes. He was happy to throw my admittedly disgusting duds in with his for nuthin'. I insisted on buying the soap, but as it turned out, the soap machine was broken, and there was a bottle of free detergent sitting on the counter. Sweet!

GoodDeeds immersed himself in his Kindle so I walked a block to a coffee house for a brew. I was pondering some of the worlds more intractable problems when a woman at a nearby table said, "Are you Badger?" I answered in the affirmative, and asked her how she knew who I was, and she said it was the New Yorker I was carrying. Talk about an eye for detail!

Her name is AwesomePossum. She'd gotten off the trail because she wasn't sure of the point of it all but had decided to do Virginia to give the trail another chance. I was taken by the fact that she'd read my journal and shared it with family members, but my laundry was due out of the dryer, and I had no idea where GoodDeeds was staying, so I had to get back. With any luck, I'll hear the rest of her story somewhere up the trail.

The open question of the day is, "Is Damascus the trail friendliest town on the AT?" I can't say. I've heard rumors of other towns, and Hot Springs certainly was nice. Certainly, you can't swing a dead cat here on Laurel Street without hitting a church, so they're in good shape in that respect. If by chance you do miss a church, you're sure to hit a bicycle rental shop. Damascus is situated on the Virginia Creeper Trail as well as the AT. The Creeper is a long section of a rail-to-trail conversion that attracts a steady stream of chuffing, sweating cyclists.

I encountered a Dairy King (yes King, not Queen) on my walk about town. My query after a malted milk netted a blank stare so I ordered one of those half-vanilla half-chocolate ice cream cones. The sign may have said Ice Kream. I'm not sure. In any event, what I got was a grainy brown and white striped concoction of indistinguishable flavors. Just so it wouldn't be a complete loss, I told the server my cone needed more salt. There was another quizzical look, but I stood my ground, and got a handful of salt packets. Salt in manageable quantities is difficult to come by on the trail. My point in all of this is to say that hikers need rich foods, and ice milk really doesn't qualify. There oughta be an ordinance or something.

There are three outfitters in town, a definite trail friendly plus. I visited all of them, and all were helpful, and in one case indulgent. I forgot to get fuel, but with little prompting, the outfitter that runs the hostel where I'm staying re-opened his store to give me a few ounces of alcohol. Thanks Mount Rogers Outfitters.

Back in the food department, the most popular restaurant is Quincy's which offers a decent, if pedestrian hiker friendly fare. It's definitely the favorite hiker hangout, but I longed, as I often do, for something more. As luck would have it, an inn, restaurant, and conference center has just started its test run in a converted mill on Beaver Creek.

There I was served a steak with mashed potatoes, and grilled asparagus — yes, a genuine green vegetable — on a terrace overlooking the millpond. It was the rarest medium steak I've ever had, but it was good.

It's a five-day hike to my next re-supply. When I checked out the Dollar General in the middle of town, it had been picked clean of hiker staples like bricks of cheese. Is that why everybody was so anxious to get here? Moreover, if there are any fresh vegetables at the DG, they're on the executive committee. My only option was to walk a mile to a new super market at the edge of town, but it was worth the trip.

So, friendliest? That judgment will have to wait, but Damascus, with its flowering trees, manicured lawns, and welcoming demeanor was certainly a pleasant place to visit.

—

We've gone from sub-freezing nights, and cool days to balmy nights, and 85-degree days, and it is not good. It means carrying much more water, and suffering a lot. Today I had to make what used to be an easy 1100 ft. climb, and it took forever. I felt like I was drinking enough water, but when I got here, I drank over a liter and a half before I felt that I'd had enough.

At least the nights will be better. I have the tarp propped up with my hiking poles so that I'm getting a nice breeze coming through.

I ran into GoodDeeds on my way out of town this morning. He was headed into town, which struck me as odd. It turns out someone accused him of smoking weed at the hostel where he was staying.

The police were called, his pack was searched but nothing was found. I asked him where he *actually* hid the stuff, and he said, "Aw, come on man, I didn't have anything!" Anyway, the upshot was that he was allowed to remain at the hostel, but he was offended, and left to camp in the woods with some section hikers. I met them on my hike out. They thought Deeds was a good guy if a bit of a character. Tonight at dinner, the speculation amongst those who'd stayed at the same hostel was that Mr. Deeds did indeed go to town as it were, but speculation is all it was.

When I stopped for lunch at Saunders Shelter, I read my first account of a bear sighting this year in the shelter log. EagleEye, whom I've met, and whose lovely wife carried treats to the top of Roan Mountain for several of us hikers encountered a sow and three cubs on the side trail to Saunders. He hikes with his dog, which immediately sensed the presence of evil, and sent them packing into the woods. Tonight I'm hanging my hammock at Lost Mountain Shelter.

—

I got up early this morning to hike as far as possible before it got hot. The weather cooperated too, staying a little cooler, and breezier. I made good progress, and as lunchtime approached, I was nearing Highway 600, and Elk Gardens. The people who hand out food to hikers have trained me not to sit down for lunch without first noting any upcoming road crossings, and holding off eating until the crossing is reached.

I did as I've been trained and came upon HemlockMuppet handing out drinks, cookies, and fruit. Everyone else who'd stayed at Lost

Mountain Shelter the previous night either was already there or showed up shortly after I did.

When the food was gone, just about everyone bolted up the trail to whatever pressing trail appointments they had, but as it was lunch time, I sat in the shade, and ate two big salami, and cheese sandwiches while enjoying the views.

I decided not to stay at a shelter, but to camp in the Grayson Highlands, which were said to be beautiful. They are without question, beautiful. They are windswept and for the most part treeless which presents a problem when one's abode is a hammock. I considered going to ground, but eventually came upon a grove of a few gnarled pines where someone had camped before as evinced by a fire ring, and some petrifying socks lying next to it.

The wind was again bothersome, but at least there was no forest litter to be blown into my food. After I ate I built a small fire to get rid of my burnable trash, and, I hope, to warn off any marauding animals. I threw in the petrifying socks for good measure. I've always hung my food out of reach of the bears, but tonight the nearest suitable tree is miles away so the food is coming inside with me. It will hang at the foot, and my bear repellent spray will hang at the head end of the hammock. I've never heard this technique recommended anywhere, but what's a guy to do? Now the fire is out, and I'm tucked in for the night, and watching the trickle of hikers still wending their way Northward not twenty feet from my little camp, oblivious to my presence.

—

No bears showed up to test my food protection plan and the wind didn't blow hard enough to pull out the tarp stakes although I was worried that it would several times. A couple of the wild ponies, a mare, and her foal watched me eat breakfast from a distance of about five feet. I'm guessing they were looking for a handout.

Yes, everything was just peachy until lunchtime when I noticed my water and filter were missing. Not knowing where they were, I decided against going back. Once I got to Hurricane Mountain Shelter, half a dozen hikers passed through saying they'd seen the filter at Wise Shelter but not knowing who it belonged to, they left it. I asked a couple of southbound hikers to let north bounders know that they could bring the filter ahead to Partnership Shelter. I also left a note in the next shelter's log with the same information. Two of the hikers I met saw the entry. Now if only a south bounder sees it, and carries the message back to Wise. I don't have a lot of hope but sometimes the stars line up, and good things happen.

I rushed here to beat the rain. I built a fire, and managed to boil three liters of water which should satisfy tomorrow's needs. I also collected half a liter of rain running off my tarp for drinking this evening. So, there is no crisis looming. I know many people who aren't treating their water, and haven't gotten sick, but I know irony wouldn't allow me to do likewise.

—

It was still raining this morning. With many machinations to keep everything dry, (sort of) it took an extra thirty minutes to pack up. BabySteps came up on me just before lunch, and we hiked into Trimpi Shelter together. She's a theater major, but she doesn't want that to be her day job so she's on the trail to think about what she'll do with her life.

A few other hikers wandered in during lunch. One of them went into hysterics when he caught sight of my rain chaps. Apparently his only experience with chaps has been at Gay Pride events. He caught his breath between fits of laughter long enough to query, "Are those ass-less chaps?" I was inclined to point out that all chaps are "ass-less", that's what makes them chaps, but was so put off by his puerile demeanor that I feigned cluelessness, and went about my business.

I was first to leave Trimpi. I reached the site where I'd planned to camp around three PM. It was early and still raining so I decided to keep moving. It was easy going; I made it to Partnership Shelter — setting another personal best for daily mileage (19.7) — which is known for having pizza delivery.

Tempting as that was, I called a cab for town so I could get an early re-supply, and get some miles in tomorrow. While I was waiting, a young woman asked me if I'd like a ride. I passed that ethical test with some difficulty, and waited for the cab. I checked into the Econo-lodge, and did my laundry in the sink. Now I'm watching Nature while my joints seize up.

—

I couldn't find my clothes bag when I was packing up in my room this morning. I never did find it. If this disturbing pattern of misplacing things continues, I'll walk into Harper's Ferry with a knife and a camp towel loincloth ... if I'm lucky.

I took the bus downtown. Busses here will divert to pick people up at their homes and businesses so

I got to see a lot of Marion. What I saw were mostly well kept, cottage like homes, and many shuttered businesses. Jan told me this corner of the state is enduring hard times, and I found little evidence to the contrary

I hitched back to the trail at 2 PM and took my time hiking to Chatfield Shelter to give my legs a break. GoodDeeds was here, having passed me on the trail, but he disappeared right after he got a call from MellowYellow, his trail girlfriend.

Half a dozen guys drifted in during the next couple of hours. I know all of them, but I can't remember their names. That didn't stop us from having a long and friendly conversation about everything, and nothing.

—

I got up at five, and was on the trail as soon as it was light enough to navigate. It took me two hours to get to the I-81 interchange at Atkins, VA. I looked into the window of the little restaurant next to the Exxon station, and the waitress smiled at me. At that point, it would have been rude not to order something don't you think? I went in, and had French toast and coffee while I called Jan.

Then it was off on a marathon march to Knot Maul. I moved along at a good clip, but I wore out with a few miles to go. I didn't think I'd have the strength to climb over Brushy Mountain when I came across a cooler full of cold drinks. I had a grape soda, and that got me over the mountain to Knot Maul Shelter. I made my dinner, and while I was eating it, SaltBomb showed up with my water filter!

The two south-bounders I'd met relayed my instructions to him, and he chased me for three days to deliver it. SaltBomb is the guy in the kilt standing on the trail next to Laurel Fork in my photos. So the stars lined up after all.

I passed the 25% mark sometime during this day. Rain is forecast for the weekend with snow in the higher elevations.

—

The weather system that was predicted moved in, and started raining on me but I put a stop to that by donning my rain gear. This works with better than chance odds for me.

My plan was to stop at a campsite at the fourteen-mile mark, but the cool weather had me feeling pretty comfortable so I marched right along to Jenkins Shelter. I've been trying to put on some big miles to make sure I can rendezvous with my friend Heinrich in Pearisburg next week. I may be overdoing it because the knees have been complaining nearly constantly and my legs seem increasingly stiff, but by my calculation, I can take it easy now, and easily make it to the designated meeting point.

I got here around seven PM. Everyone had finished cooking so I had all the room I needed to fix a big pot of red beans, and rice. As I was doing that, a woman arrived, and inquired if there was room for more campers in the shelter. The answer that came back was "No" which was technically correct, the shelter's advertised capacity had been reached, but one or two more spaces could have been opened up had people been willing to scrunch together. That's what happened all the time with my first cohort. We'd be packed in so tight we'd be legally married in ten states. I was disappointed not to see the one for all, all for one dynamic repeated here.

—

It rained, then I hiked. I got to Bland around noon just as I was overtaken by Hotsauce. We hitched into town and ordered a couple of foot longs at the Subway's. Hotsauce left a Next Gen Prosthetics research position to hike the trail. Made sense to me. He plans to enter medical school in the fall. Made more sense.

He hitched back to the trail, and I got a room at Big Walker Hotel out by the interstate to await the morning opening of the post office. Bland doesn't have a lot, but it does have free Wi-Fi, a social program that seems incongruous amongst the American Owned signs, and businesses incorporating "freedom" in their titles.

But that's about all it's got; no Laundromat. I couldn't even find alcohol for my stove; in a trail town. My last hope is the NAPA parts store that won't open until tomorrow. They may have some gas line antifreeze that will do in a pinch. Just in case, I cancelled plans for hot breakfasts to stretch what I have.

I only need to do 14 miles or less a day to Pearisburg. I'm looking forward to meeting some new hikers as they pass.

—

I stuck my head out the hotel door this morning to gauge the temperature and saw a few random snowflakes. By the time I'd walked from the interstate to the middle of town, it was snowing hard. I'm glad I ventured into the town proper. I was beginning to think the town was inhabited solely by unknowledgeable, incurious, indifferent people. I was informed of two sources of alcohol.

Alcohol stoves are popular with hikers owing to their lightweight. Fuel is supplied by outfitters, and other stores, which purchase denatured alcohol by the gallon, add a modest markup of around 700% to cover expenses, and resell it to hikers by the ounce. The owner of the convenience store by the interstate reasoned that he'd make twice as much money with a 1400% markup. When I asked for some, he said it hadn't been moving, so he didn't restock when his supply ran out. The NAPA store didn't sell alcohol by the ounce, but a hiker had bought a quart there, taken what he needed, and left the rest with instructions that it be given free to other hikers.

I ate breakfast at the only restaurant downtown. Due to a misunderstanding, I was served an order of biscuits, and gravy, an awful looking dish consisting of two biscuits smothered in thick, gray gravy. It wasn't as bad as it looked, but it's not something I'll be ordering often.

My package wasn't at the post office so I forwarded it one hundred miles up the trail to Catawba, and hitched to the trail.

—

It snowed hard, and the wind blew hard, but I much prefer snow to rain because I don't need to wear my rain gear. There was more accumulation as I got higher. I was overtaken by EagleEye, and his dog just before noon, and we hiked together for the rest of the day. Everyone else at the shelter he came from had decided to wait out the storm in the shelter. That proved unnecessary as the accumulation maxed out at less than an inch, and had melted by day's end. EagleEye's dog Jack flushed a turkey hen, which was nesting not ten feet from the trail. The nest was loaded with big brown speckled eggs. Hundreds of people have probably walked past that nest without seeing it. The storm system is supposed to move away during the night, but not before it delivers its lowest temperatures yet. I'm warm in my hammock here at Jenny Knob Shelter in my winter sleeping bag thanks to the timely advice from *The Sage of Hot Springs*.

—

Once again, benign trail conditions got the better of me. I had hiked the 14.5 miles to Wapiti Shelter by three PM. Laura Susan Ramsay, and Robert Mountford Jr. were murdered in this shelter in 1981. The place was deserted, and given its provenance, I opted to hike another six miles to Wood's Hole Hostel. Arriving at dusk, I trudged across the yard in the failing light, and was about to knock on the front door when it was opened by a beautiful young woman who said, "We were just sitting down to supper. Would you like us to set a place for you?"

Woods Hole is listed as a "don't miss" in the guidebooks, and I pretty much agree with that assessment. With the exception of the Hiker Hostel, hostels haven't placed a high priority on cleanliness. This place is like a good hotel except the guests are asked to help out with things like clearing the table, and making their beds.

The table was piled high with excellent fare. There was plenty to eat which at this juncture is saying something. Halfway through the meal,

SaltBomb darkened the front door and was ushered to the table. I was happy he'd made it to this "piece of heaven" but taken aback by ensuing events. It seems that he had hiked up with EagleEye and The GourmetGirls who were engaged in one of the AT's many "challenges". There's the Maryland Challenge in which hikers attempt to cross the state of Maryland (40 mi) in a single day, and the Half-Gallon Challenge in which hikers are challenged to eat a Half-Gallon of ice cream at the AT's halfway point. I don't remember the name of this particular challenge, but it involved hiking 24 miles in 24 hours carrying and drinking a beer an hour. So SaltBomb, apparently a bit of a moralist, ratted them out to the innkeeper who is a bit of a moralist herself and wouldn't let them inside for dinner. She served them on the front porch, which would have made for some elegant dining save for the plummeting temperature.

Unfamiliar as I am with matters alcohol, I still seem to recall from the movies in high school health class that a beer an hour isn't a lot. Their behavior certainly didn't seem out of the ordinary, and by that, I mean that they were the same considerate, attentive kids who offer old guys with stiff joints their seat without prompting. As long as we're passing around moral codes for others to sample, perhaps SaltBomb could adopt the one EagleEye lives by, namely, "Mind your own business."

—

I was up at my usual hour, and breakfast wasn't served until eight. With nothing better to do, I shredded potatoes for hash browns. Breakfast started with a ritual in which we all held hands around the table, and said what we were thankful for. There were many "awesome" things people were

68

thankful for. When my turn came, I was ready to say I was thankful for people who reserve "awesome" for when they find their jaws hanging below their waists, but in the interest of comity, I let it go. I said I was thankful for "tolerance". That garnered patronizing smiles all around.

I noticed the occasional discarded beer can on the trail that morning. I won't pick up anything that isn't edible unless it has negative weight, but SaltBomb, being young and fit, tossed them in his pack and handed them to Resource (one of the GourmetGirls) when he overtook her. They were sheepishly accepted without comment. OK, so maybe a beer an hour is more than some hikers should allow themselves.

The vertical drop of nearly half a mile to Pearisburg was brutal on the knees. I was lame by the end of the descent. I hobbled into town, and got a room. My knees started to work better once I got rid of the pack. I ran into EagleEye who'd squared things with SaltBomb earlier in the day, which is good. They're both nice boys. We hit the Mexican restaurant across the street from the Plaza Hotel along with Whitewater for margaritas, and burritos. The other gourmet girl, Whoop, was disappointed that she didn't know we were going for Mexican.

With nothing to do but wait for Heinrich, I took a walk about town this morning. The downtown is small, it has a couple of restaurants, an antique store among other businesses, and a number of empty store fronts of businesses likely usurped by the Wal-Mart. Interestingly, American Owned has been supplanted by The Ten Commandments posted prominently in many businesses. I think that's good. We can't have people forgetting themselves and tipping vending machines over on surly store clerks or coveting the buxom wife of the man in the adjoining motel room. For an absentminded person like me, these reminders are, well, a godsend.

The largest employer in town is an acetate plant that was visible from the AT on the ridge. EagleEye said the plant was open and running full bore when he was descending around two AM the other day. The principal product is cigarette filters.

It rained all morning. The Plaza Motel is a hiker friendly place; it maintains a hiker box, and does laundry for free so there were quite a few hikers there, and it looked like most of them planned to stay for another day. I don't think that will help much because rain is forecast for the rest of the week. The GourmetGirls must have felt the same way because they disappeared into the mid-morning downpour.

Checkout time was eleven, so it was off to the Dairy Queen to nurse a meal until Heinrich arrived, which he did just after noon. By the time we'd gotten organized, the rain had stopped, and we began our hike with a long climb. The rain held off until after we'd reached Rice Field Shelter and finished dinner which we did quickly because I spilled half the mac, and cheese. We also had a big pot of broccoli that Jan sent with Heinrich, a first for me on the trail. We had made good time, and aside from needing some ibuprofen, Heinrich said he felt pretty good when we turned in.

—

The rest of the spilled mac and cheese was cleaned up by the shelter mice during the night. They stored what they couldn't eat in one of Salt Bomb's shoes. They used his other shoe for a latrine. Heinrich stayed in the shelter too but had the foresight to hang his shoes from a nail, and came away clean.

A lot of people are rolling into Pine Swamp Branch Shelter late because they came all the way from Pearisburg today. I'm enjoying the leisurely pace we've set. I decided to stay in the shelter because there were a number of widow makers above the nearby hammock sites, and I didn't want to set up far from the shelter.

—

I should have known better. My night in the shelter was a night in hell. When the pain became unbearable, I'd shift to a new position, and wait for the new pain to overcome me. I don't think I slept more than four hours. Never again, or at least not until I forget how bad it was the way I forgot the shelters in the Smokies.

The day didn't start too badly but by mid-morning, we were experiencing a downpour with hail. It was 38 degrees. So we suffered with cold hands, and wet feet for a few hours, but the rain stopped at noon, and the weather got progressively better all day.

Now we're sitting here in front of a fire that EagleEye built at Warspur Shelter. His dog Jack is cavorting out on the grass with Elke, another German shepherd that hiked in with two sisters. Heinrich and I had a concoction of powdered margarita mix, and alcohol for after dinner drinks. We're feeling pretty mellow, and are hammocking (early) on the lawn tonight.

—

Every day on the trail is a personal best for longest re-supplied hike for me. Today was also a personal best for Heinrich. Sadly, it was also his last day. He'll be off to his conference tomorrow. I enjoyed the company of my good friend. I know it was difficult for him, but he never complained, and always kept up.

We climbed the last hill after the shelter, recovered Heinrich's car, and drove to Blacksburg where we were greeted by my daughter, her husband, and my sister Emilie, and her husband. We spent the rest of the day engaged in airy persiflage at my daughter's home, and at a great dinner as guests of sister and brother-in-law.

Tomorrow it's look for some new trail shoes to replace my winter hiking boots, re-supply, and get back on the trail.

—

I saw Heinrich off at 6:30, and ate breakfast with my daughter who then took me out to the Kroger's for re-supply and then to Backcountry for some new shoes. I got some light trail runners. They didn't have any in a wide so I took a chance on regular width. Daughter said she'd bring my old boots forward to Catawba if there was a problem. So far some minor pains but pretty good; much lighter than my winter boats.

Sister and husband took us to a barbecue place for lunch. Then they drove me back to the trail. Maintainers had been working at cutting brush away from the trail including small saplings. The saplings had been cut at an acute angle about a foot above the ground leaving stumps that would impale any hiker unfortunate enough to fall on one.

I missed seeing the Keffer Oak AGAIN. (We'd hiked here previously). I asked TrailMix about it this evening. He said he saw the Oak when he passed it, but it was easy to miss; not all that imposing and the sign was partially obscured. It threatened rain all afternoon, but I kept it at bay by wearing my rain cape. I watched for the wasp nest that got us last summer, but never saw one. It looked like a lot of brush cutting has gone on since we traversed back then.

I got to Niday Shelter at 7:30. I recognized the hiking sisters, their German shepherd Elke, and some section hikers. Most everyone else here had already eaten, and they had a fire going so I put out the bag of marshmallows I'd carried up, and invited everyone to partake. Aside from TrailMix who's in his twenties, everyone looked to be over 40. All of the women, and TrailMix went for the treat like flies for a horse apple, but none of the other men did. I haven't figured that one out. I did manage to get Johannes, a German, to try roasting one after he watched the others for a while. He pronounced it good, but didn't have another.

I had a great meal that was a mixture of Knorr Steak Fajita rice, cous cous, and dried bell peppers which my sister gave me as a going away present.

It's warm, and clammy in my hammock. I'm only using my sleeping bag liner for the moment. Temperature management is going to be a dicey walk between staying warm, and not so warm that I sweat.

May, 689 Miles

I saw more lady slippers today than in the rest of my life I think. The rhododendrons and mountain laurel are also in early bloom. I can't wait for full bloom when there will be long corridors lined with beautiful flowers.

I'm covering the same ground that my wife and I hiked last year albeit at a faster pace. We took two days to cover what I hiked today. The place where we lost the trail on the descent from Dragon's Tooth is now marked with copious blazes about three feet apart owing, I assume, to the email sent to the Roanoke Trails Club last year pointing out that many hikers had gone astray on that descent. At lunch, I dropped my knife on my foot. The tip of the blade penetrated my shoe, my sock, and my foot. Please note that this waited until I was wearing brand new socks, and shoes to happen. The nick was small but deep. There's a one-inch bruise around the wound. In the afternoon, I saw my first copperhead. It was small; 18 inches maybe. I flicked him into the woods with my hiking pole.

Now I'm at Four Pines Hostel — a bare bones place with cots, a cat, and a bathroom in a three-car garage. Joe, the owner, drives people to the store, and the post office. Payment is via donation box. I had a pizza from the store, and I'm showered and ready for bed. One of the guys here missed the turnoff on Dragon's Tooth despite the virtual dotted line of blazes. Tomorrow hostel owner Joe will take me to the post office then it's back to the trail for a two day walk to Daleville.

—

Joe drove me to the Post Office this morning, and, lo and behold, they had my package. Package in hand, we returned to the hostel where I packed and was on my way. The highway 311 crossing came around noon so I held off on lunch until I got there to see if there was any trail magic to be had; nada, so I hung my socks, and shoes on a guardrail to dry in the sun while I made lunch in the shade nearby. As I was doing that, a man who'd hiked earlier in the day took an interest in my travels, and ended up giving me a soft drink, and some candy.

Speaking of candy, my Hershey's drops melted partially yesterday so I moved them from the lid of my pack to the side pouch next to my water bottle. I also put three snickers minis in there, and nothing melted in the heat of the day.

As I started up the trail after lunch, a day hiker asked me if I could identify the large bird circling overhead.

"It's a vulture." I said.

"Are you sure? It's so majestic."

"Yeah I'm sure. He's been dogging me for a week!"

It took her a moment to assess my obvious accumulation of years, then she laughed.

I hiked up to McAffee Knob, and helped a few young couples by taking their picture on the outcropping. They took my picture too, but not the traditional edge sitting, feet dangling one. Anyone who wants to see that can look at the photo in my

2011 AT journal. Then it was on to Tinker Cliffs where I lost time following a false trail, and more time building a barrier so others wouldn't make the same mistake. As it happens, I ran into others who missed this turn both before and after I built the barrier. They wound up missing the beautiful view from Tinker Cliffs. Then it was on Lambert's Meadow Shelter where I found a good group finishing dinner. I hadn't met any of them except StrayDog whom I'd shared a beer with at Four Pines.

I got an email asking about the pros, and cons of hammocking. Well, it's been said that those who tent are a bunch of slack-jawed cretins, but that is completely false, misleading, and mean spirited. The hammock is confining but much more comfortable than the hard ground in my opinion. My Hennessy Hyper-light Backpacker weighs 1 lb 10 oz. which is lighter than most one-man tents, and it's made of durable fabric that's held up well. One-man tents that are lighter are often made of very thin, weaker materials. They may not last long. With a hammock, you'll always have a camp chair, something many campers long for, but are unable or unwilling to carry. A hammock can be set up anywhere there are trees. I've slept on slopes, and over rocks, and bogs. Early on in this endeavor, a fellow hiker related his experience pitching his tent on a slope. It rained, and the water provided enough lubrication to send him gliding into a ravine. That's a pretty wild ride to be taking at 3 AM. He also lost half his tent stakes. I hope that helps.

—

I really didn't intend to stay in Daleville. I was here before noon. I would have been even earlier but I stopped for pie. I used the free Wi-Fi at McDonald's to upload photos, and stuff. As I was finishing up, a woman asked me if I was a through-hiker. As it happened, I was. Her name is Nancy Balchik, a saint if ever there was one. Her son is hiking the AT. He's in Hot Springs at the moment.

Nancy offered to help me get through my town chores. She took me to the barbershop, the outfitter for permethrins, and the Kroger's for re-supply. We talked as we went. I made an awkward attempt to assuage her concerns for her son's safety, which probably made things worse. I pointed out that my encounter with the dullard with the confederate flag hat ended well. Smart!

With so much help, it should've been easy to get out of town but treating my clothes took longer than I planned, and I forgot to get cheese, putting me at a serious calorie deficit so I checked in to the HoJo's.

The hike into town was all down hill through familiar territory. There were more blooms on the mountain laurel, and there was a continuous trill from every direction signaling the emergence of the 17-year locust.

I'll be up at five, and I'll leave right after the 6 AM free breakfast. The trail is down the block, so it will be a quick getaway.

—

After hiking through rhododendron groves for two months, I finally came to some in full bloom today. I hope the photos I took do them justice. They give the trail a festive, welcoming air.

It took most of the morning for the sound of the cicadas to supplant the roar of Interstate Highway

81. I reached the second shelter of the day around 3:30. I was tired so I took a half hour nap. It might have been longer if one of the section hikers planning to spend the night had used his inside voice. In any event, I awoke refreshed, and ready to hike some more so I did another 7 miles to get to Bobblet's Gap Shelter. So did StrayDog who came in right behind me. He'd carried a steak up from Daleville, and offered me a bite in exchange for a glass of Tang.

Good old Tang!

After dinner, StrayDog made a sack out of his tarp, and stuffed it with leaves to make a mattress. Neat!

—

When I left Bobblet's this morning, StrayDog was hard at work fixing his $224 Asolo boots, which had been attacking his Achilles tendon. I've never been a fan. I purchased a pair once. They were so uncomfortable I sent them back. I've met a number of people who've gotten serious blisters from their Asolos. I think they should get out of the boot business. Their corporate moniker is an ideal aptronym for a number of products. How about *Asol-o toroidal suppositories*? or: *Asol-os, the heart friendly breakfast cereal for difficult personalities* or my personal favorite: *As-so-lo, the toilet designed with tots in mind.* StrayDog overtook me later in the morning. He's in his late twenties or early thirties. He looks vaguely like Brad Pit. He has a femur length scar on his right leg where surgeons opened him up to repair some motorcycle carelessness.

He passed me, wobbly game leg kicking unnaturally to the side, huge pack lurching this way and that, and disappeared down the trail. I wondered if there is anyone or thing on this trail that is slower than I am.

It threatened to rain all morning. I grew so weary of donning, and removing the rain gear that I gave it up, ignoring the odd rain shower that passed. The cicada seem to have a preferred altitude, which I climbed and descended through a couple of times. Their collective chirp was almost deafening at times.

When I reached Bryant Ridge Shelter around 3 PM, StrayDog and Hoot from the previous shelter were there. It had just started to rain in earnest, and they had decided to spend the night to avoid the climb up Floyd Mountain in the rain. The idea had some appeal. The shelter is new. It has multiple levels, windows, benches, and a picnic table under roof. However, despite the attractive architecture, a shelter is just a mouse-infested box with hard floors. I checked my book. The climb was 1700 feet in 3.1 miles. Nuthin'! It nearly met railroad max grade spec. I rolled out my mat, and took a 45-minute nap. Then I geared up, and climbed. I was on top in an hour and a half and at my campsite a few minutes later. It's a little clammy in my hammock, what with clouds blowing through and all, but I'll make do.

—

It was cloudy, and cool all morning, good for hiking but the trails weren't all that great. I did run across some hillsides covered with trillium. I took a photo which I'm sure won't do them justice.

I had a lunch of cheese & pepperoni wraps. Pepperoni because Kroger didn't have any small summer sausage. Neither meat is entirely satisfactory. The salmon packets that Heinrich left with me were pretty good, but it was impossible to avoid getting some of the juice on me. I could wash it off my hands, but it stayed on my clothes pretty well as the keen interest paid me by the Four Pines cat testified. If he was interested, other animals would be interested so I'm still looking for a high calorie meat filling that will keep for several days.

Hoot caught up with me after lunch, and we hiked together until he reached his goal of 17 miles. He was educated in geo-science, but spent most of his career as a machinist. He seems to have read a newspaper once in a while, something many people I've met out here have not.

I soldiered on for another hour before I found this campsite. There's no water here, but I was prepared for that. I carried water from the site where I left Hoot.

I built a fire after dinner to let the wild animals know there is an invincible human camped here. Now it's starting to blow, and rain is falling. I'm not worried. The tarp is tied to trees, and logs. I'm glad the rain held off until I was finished with my outside chores.

—

It rained most of the night, and it may as well have rained all day because the mist was so heavy that anything exposed to it got wet. What isn't wet is clammy, and sticky. My sleeping bag liner feels like fly paper, and everything stinks.

That last sentence may confuse some people. What I meant was everything stinks more than usual. I've heard that a thru-hiker, a section hiker, and a day hiker were thrown into a pigsty to see who could tolerate the stench the longest. The day hiker came out on the first day, the section hiker came out on the second day, and the pigs bolted on the third. Yeah, I know. Tired joke retread!

When I put my pack on this morning, I noticed some critter bites in the waist straps. It was probably a raccoon because the straps were too high off the ground for it to have been mice. That's another species that's going on my list. Hoot caught up with me in the morning, and we hiked together until we came to Matt's Creek Shelter where he stopped to eat breakfast. He caught me again at the James River, but I let him pass. I'd slipped on a greasy patch, and my left knee felt like I might have stretched something. I took it easy until I was pretty sure it was okay.

In the afternoon, Resource, one of the GourmetGirls hiked with me for a while. I was surprised to see her behind me since the last time I saw them, they were disappearing into the rain as they left Pearisburg a day ahead of me. She's taking the semester off from Lewis and Clark to hike. She entertained me with stories about her studies abroad in Africa until we reached the top of a climb, and ran into some other hikers. She stayed to wait for her hiking partner Whoop, and I continued to Punchbowl Shelter which was packed to capacity when I arrived. A couple more hikers arrived, and asked if there was any room. This time, everyone agreed to scrunch together. There was some irony in this because the newcomers had nothing to offer but stony silence the last time this situation came up, and they were being asked if there was any room at the inn.

Personal bests: I've completed the first third of my AT hike. When I make my triumphal entry into

Buena Vista tomorrow, I'll have completed my longest hike yet without re-supply. 79.3 miles!![1]

—

I was on the trail by seven. I stopped at the first spring I found with good flow to replace the greenish water I collected at Punchbowl. I'd dumped out my water bottles when I noticed what looked like a tampon in the spring pool. I thought, "Is this some kind of lame joke?" Upon closer inspection, I could see that the tampon was actually the carcass of a mouse! It was then and there that I resolved to end my hike immediately, and dedicate the rest of my life to sitting before the hearth, margarita in one hand, and large print book in the other. Later, as I was refilling my bottles from a cleaner source, I decided against quitting in favor of soldiering on. I'm a flip-flopper you see.

Hoot caught up with me as he always has, and we hiked together for the rest of the morning. I mentioned the spring. He said he hadn't taken on water there but two section hikers did. We decided that if we saw them again — we did — the less said the better.

I said goodbye to a sodden Hoot who was staying on the trail, and boarded a shuttle to Buena Vista. The locals pronounce it Byouna Vista. The town has one of the more charming main streets so far on the trail. Shade trees and vintage architecture make all the difference. Unfortunately, the demise of some of the local manufacturing base has resulted in far too many empty storefronts, and an influx of

---

[1] My current record is 105 mi. in the Shenandoah National Park Nov. 2014 without re-supply. It helps to go ultra-light

The Badger and Hoot

businesses inappropriate for casual shopping; dentist offices, and similar. The town is trying to build a trail friendly reputation. Michael Ohleger of the Uncorked wine store is spearheading the effort. He gave me some good advice about food and lodging.

The walk to the Food Lion consisted of the occasional sidewalk interspersed with free fire zones. I bought mostly the customary stuff, but included a slice of ham, fresh spinach, and mashed potatoes, and a paper plate for a proper first night's meal. If you're wondering how I got them to sell me a single paper plate, I didn't.

An email asked how I was able to leave my dog behind. My wife is taking care of her. It's really her dog. Another asked how I hang my pack from my hammock; a lot more carefully since the forest vermin attacked a waist strap. I hook the lid over the suspension at the entry end so I can get to the contents easily if I need to during the night. I now tie the belt straps up so they don't hang so close to the ground.

—

It took a half hour to score a ride from a woman who works near the trailhead. There was nothing extraordinary about the hiking in the morning. It rained all afternoon, and got progressively colder. I became concerned about the adequacy of my summer gear. I decided to cook dinner when I got to Seely Woodworth Shelter. Recall the ham, spinach, and mashed potatoes purchased yesterday. Only one pot, and burner meant sequential courses, but the dinner was great anyway. After dinner, I pressed on for two miles to this campsite. It's windy and cold so I donned my rain gear and shirt before retiring. I'm very comfortable except for the annoying wind noise. It's nice to have a portable cozy cottage.

—

Well, my cozy shelter got less cozy. The temperature dropped lower, and the wind blew harder until I was worried that the flapping of the tarp might cause it to fray. I got out, and put weights on the lines, and the stakes. I was uncomfortable for most of the night, but I never shivered so I didn't resort to hand warmers. When morning came, I didn't bother with stuff sacks or putting everything in its place. I just jammed everything in the pack, and hit the trail.

I got to The Priest Shelter around ten where I cleaned up my pack, and cooked breakfast out of the wind. The descent from The Priest to the Tye River took 'til noon so I ate lunch on a sunny rock in the river before climbing first to Harper's Creek Shelter where I took a nap, and then on up to Maupin Field Shelter. It was a long climb; about half of it in the dark, which made for slow going on a rocky twisty trail. It's dead calm now, so I hope to catch up on my sleep.

—

It got into the thirties, and I didn't sleep well. As I walked today, I formulated a new insulation strategy. Tonight I folded the pad double under my torso, brought my pack inside, and placed it under my legs. Before I wrote a word, I fell asleep for six hours, and awoke sweating. That's a sign that something is working a little better.

I didn't much enjoy the day's hike. I was exhausted, and light-headed, and the trail was uncooperative. It was one rockslide after another. My new shoes, while light, and convenient, are not as comfortable as my winter boots. I've had to use band-aids and moleskin on hot spots to prevent blisters. Another annoyance is the extra ventilation, which lets, in extra dirt.

As lunchtime rolled around, I came upon a cliff overlooking the Shenandoah Valley. I joined a day hiker in his late seventies who'd shot past me some time earlier. He was hiking with a group but he'd gotten far ahead of it. He said he had a naturally rapid gait, and he never suffered from stiffness. I looked at my arthritic knuckles, my knees that would have me weighing the pros, and cons of squatting to pick up a thousand dollar bill, and fought back a nascent urge to toss him off the cliff. He'd had an interesting career as a research chemist, once working on a project to turn oil into a low cost food product. High oil prices put an end to that. Now he's auditing astronomy, and particle physics courses at the University of Virginia. I enjoyed our chat. He told me the trail would be more benign in the afternoon. It did smooth out quite a bit.

There are three other hikers camped here at Paul C. Wolfe Shelter; two of them Iraq war veterans. The dinner conversation went mostly to the war. One told of how in the early days of the invasion there was a supply screw-up, and they went without food for four days. Eventually they turned to the inhabitants of a nearby village for chickens, and vegetables. That was before the insurgency took hold. I listened until exhaustion and cold drove me to bed.

—

Ten hours of sleep did me good. I awoke refreshed, and ready to rocket into Rockfish Gap where I would meet my wife Jan at the visitor's center. I fortified myself with coffee and a big bowl of granola and got going. It was downhill all the way; figuratively speaking.

The knife nick on my foot has turned into a small lesion that's irritated by my shoe, and making walking difficult. The new shoes also wore a hole in another toe. I killed the pain with a couple of dashes of Neosporin-with-pain-relief and kept going. My knee, the one I worried might have injured the other day, would buckle occasionally. Knowing I couldn't rely on it really slowed me down. Putting on the miles over the last few days so I could get to the gap early wasn't the best idea I've had on this trip.

I limped into the visitors center Rockfish Gap where Jan showed up with a picnic meal that was unique in my recent experience in that it was neither rehydrated carbs nor awash in grease. The visitor's center is very hiker friendly by the way. They maintain a list of volunteers who'll drive hikers to, and around Waynesboro, have fuel, a hiker box, and lots of useful information. It had to move up the hill from the original location two years ago. The attendant told me that the move cut the number of hikers stopping in way down. Believe me; it's worth the five-minute walk up the hill.

We're at a beautiful B&B in Stanton for two days of R&R. We picked up new socks, and liners at the outfitter. Now I'm letting my wounds dry out, and waiting to see if the knee, which is noticeably larger and hotter than the other one, will get better.

—

Stanton is a great city to zero in. Despite suffering the largest population decline in the state, it has a vibrant downtown. Beverly Street and its cross streets abound with galleries, fine restaurants, shops, and theaters comfortably ensconced in late 19th century charm.

My leg ached, but it was up to the light duty of window-shopping. We enjoyed a late Mother's Day brunch, and returned to the inn to watch the season premier of Mad Men, our guilty pleasure. Tomorrow we'll pick up supplies for the walk to Loft Mountain Store in the Shenandoah National Park. I plan to make short miles for a while to help my leg out.

—

I made a big change today. I wanted to try some other drinks, but Tang always won out big time in the calorie department. Scrutiny of the labels this morning revealed that same volumes of other powdered drink mixes had the same number of calories as the big T, they just specified less mix per drink. As I understand it, these instructions aren't rigorously enforced in the wilderness, so I'm going to mix up my drinks based on calories.

Jan and I ate breakfast at the B & B, and then I re-supplied at the Kroger's on the way back to the trailhead. She dropped me off, and then she turned into a trail angel, driving a couple of hikers into Waynesboro.

My priority was to get through the day without aggravating any of my injuries. I put a brace on my knee even though I don't know if it will help. I got rid of the band-aids on my foot lesions in favor of a liquid bandage that lets the wound dry out, and I put on sock liners. The first liners were from the outfitter. They weren't very thin; more like a second pair of socks. They made my shoes feel too tight so we bought some calf length nylons forty cents a pair. They add virtually no bulk, and effectively decouple my socks from my feet so there's no rubbing. Finally, I resolved to walk at a leisurely pace.

Some combination of these things working with or against each other got me here with nothing being any worse than when I started. My left knee never let me forget that it has problems, but it didn't buckle once. The trail was toothy, and meandered, and undulated without rhyme or reason. There was a heavy mist, and visibility was limited even more by unusually dense undergrowth. I made good a mile, and a half per hour, which I thought respectable under the circumstances.

There were half a dozen people at Calf Mountain Shelter ahead of me. Most of them had taken refuge just after noon when the storm strengthened. Did I mention it's been raining since I hit the trail today? I set up my hammock close to the shelter, and got in right after dinner. I'll renew my liquid bandages, and do a little reading after that.

—

It rained until late. Then it rained harder. Then the skies opened up. I peeked out of the hammock at about three AM, and noted that I was hanging over a lake. Word filtered in tonight that the storm interrupted transportation and commerce across the region.

The weather was much better today, and trail conditions were excellent but it was difficult hiking. The shoes that the salesman said would dry out if I put them on and hiked for an hour are still wet. The liquid bandage held up though, and there's less inflammation tonight. I made better time today, but I attribute that solely to trail conditions. My knee kept sending messages to slow down.

I ran into a familiar face but couldn't remember the name until I said good morning, and he didn't reply. It was NoHear'Em. I tried to engage him in conversation about a week ago, and was ignored. I assumed he was just one of the outlying personalities that feel more at home out here than anywhere else, but later learned he's deafer than I am. So this time I yelled, and we talked for a few minutes. He has two cars. He drives one ahead, then hikes back to the other, and leapfrogs it, and hikes back again. He never has to worry about rides to town or getting from motel to store.

I reached Blackrock Hut early, but resisted the temptation to move on. A thunderstorm passed through, but it's supposed to be sunny and dry tomorrow.

—

Nothing of importance happened today. Really, nothing. The knee was its perplexing self, feeling normal, and strong one moment, and in debilitating pain the next only to feel normal seconds or tens of minutes later. It was much better I think after an NSAID I took right after lunch so I'll try a pre-emptive dose in the morning.

I stopped for lunch at Loft Mountain Wayside, home of the world's most expensive lunch. I ordered a cheeseburger. The counterman asked me what I wanted on it. I asked for lettuce ($0.31), tomato ($0.31), and onion ($0.26). I said, "What, this is a pizza parlor?" The burger fries, and chocolate milk shake came to $15.31. With prices like that, it's no wonder so few people hike the AT.

Instigator and Expediter joined me at my table. About halfway through lunch, NoHear'Em happened along. It sounded like a shouting match after that with lots of

"Who?"

"Thursday?"

"NO, THIRSTY!"

"What?"

I got to Pinefield Hut around four, and got into my hammock for some light reading. The knee was no different in the hammock, sometimes moving easily, and sometimes painfully. I ate late when I felt hungry again. Tomorrow I'll walk four miles to an intersection of the AT and Skyline Drive where I'll meet Jan, and she'll drive me for an easy re-supply. She'll drop me off, and I'll hike on to the next shelter. I'll only hike about eight miles total,

Instigator and NoHear'Em

and hope that taking it easy will help my cotton-picking knee.

—

Last night when I looked in my guidebook, the place where the trail crossed Skyline Drive was 4 miles away. When I checked this morning, it was 5.4 miles. It would take some hustling to get there by 9 am, and my gimpy leg wasn't going to make it easier.

I worked extra hard on the up slopes that don't bother my leg much, and did my best on the downs. When I walked out of the woods at 9:04, the first thing I saw was the nose of the family automobile. The second was Jan getting out of it. We drove down to the Elkton Food Lion, and bought enough food to see me out of the park, stopped at McDonald's to eat lunch, re-charge electrics, and post journal entries via the free Wi-Fi. Good old McDonald's.

Gorp (formerly known as TrailMix) walked up as Jan was dropping me off. I gave him half the hot dogs and buns I'd bought because I was pretty sure I'd only want four.

I hiked up to High Top Hut with the aid of a stiffer leg brace that Jan brought from my extensive collection. What a dismal place. The fire ring was full of garbage. There was bear scat everywhere, and the flies had some kind of international air show going on. StrayDog's log entry from five days ago said a bear stole his cooking pot. That's not surprising. He was never too big on hanging all his stuff on the bear poles. I'd planned to spend the afternoon reading there, but I couldn't stand the place after ten minutes, and moved on up here where I found a small clearing just short of a scenic overlook. I set up my shelter, and walked down to the overlook where I read my New Yorker, and chatted up hikers, and a couple of trail runners from James Madison U. I cooked on the rocks, and ate my four hot dogs with relish, onions, mustard, and catsup while gazing out over the Shenandoah Valley. Those were some dang good hot dogs.

—

The day started of with me meeting FruitLoop, half of the duo that Jan drove into Waynesboro after she dropped me off at the trailhead at Rockfish Gap. We leapfrogged throughout the day.

Eventually we landed at the Lewis Mountain Campground store with other members of her cohort including Blue, the other half of the duo that got the lift. We sat around overindulging in soft drinks, and snacks for a while. FruitLoop decided to stay at Bearfence Hut despite reported bear problems there, the rest of them decided to press on to Big Meadow. The latter being too far, and the former being too close for me, I am camping in the woods alone. I could have gone on to Big Meadow I guess, but I'm giving the leg, which performed admirably today, a break as it were.

So, I was perched on a rock finishing supper on the mountaintop when Stats, a member of FruitLoop's cohort came along and chatted me up about his plan to give his family a surprise home visit. I thought to myself that surprises like that can end up being surprising in ways unintended, but I let it lie. He ended the conversation by letting me know he'd heard what sounded like a bear crashing through the woods nearby. The information was utterly useless to me. Bears live in the park, and can show up anywhere. Useful information would be telling me how to make an effective bear trap using dental floss, and a couple of rocks. Then he told me if I hung my food, which I always do anyway, the bears wouldn't bother me. Now how could he know that? Is he one of their familiars? Are all the bears in the park members of some sort of bear reform movement? We wished each other well, and he headed off to Big Meadow. I packed up, and moved a ways down the mountain from where I'd fixed dinner. I hung my food bag following the specifications published by the park and well away from my hammock so any efforts to steal it won't disturb my sleep. My bear spray is hanging from the ridgeline of my hammock, and I have mentally rehearsed many scenarios of bear encounters. I'm happy to say that I've emerged victorious in all of them.

—

I was just nodding off last night when a screech owl that must have been perched on or near my hammock let loose an unholy howl. It was one of those rare bowel cleansing moments. I feel most fortunate that I'd attended to that task some hours earlier or it would have been an uncomfortable situation, not that it wasn't bad anyway. I spent the night never in more than a half sleep, clutching my bear repellent to my chest.

In the morning, I packed as fast as I could, and charged away from those woods, which were no less bleak and scary than the ones in The Wizard of Oz. I didn't eat breakfast until I reached the Big Meadow picnic area. The book didn't list a store there, but I found a small concession that sold sodas, and frozen snacks. I asked for a drumstick cone, and the attendant gave it to me gratis. Sweet!

It's the weekend, and the woods are lousy with day hikers. It's quite a change to go from seeing almost no one to being buttonholed every fifteen minutes or so. I ate lunch at Rock Springs Hut, the same one where Jan and I sought refuge after being viciously almost attacked by a bear a few years ago. I ate an experimental wrap filled with hard salami and cheddar. Gaak! Not good, and I have two more in my food bag. I stopped at Skyland Lodge for a soda, coffee, cookie, and a phone re-charge in the lounge before hiking to the top of this hillock campsite. I kept going on down the hill to Skyline Drive where I cooked dinner well away from camp so as not to attract bears.

It's been so long since I stayed near a shelter that I feel like a hermit. I've adjusted my planned miles so I'll land on one Monday. Tuesday it'll be out of the park, and home for a couple of zero days.

—

It was a perfect day weather wise. It was the first time I can remember it being warm enough when I awoke that extra layers to stay warm were not required. Not having to cope with the cold made it easier to pack too, and I was on the trail 15 minutes ahead of my usual time. I didn't eat breakfast until I got to the Pinnacle Picnic Area, which I had all to myself.

The weather stayed breezy and in the 70's, and the trails cooperated too. I talked to a motor cycle camper while I was eating lunch at Beahms Gap Overlook. He was leaving the park today so he left his snacks with me. His bike was whisper quiet. I was grateful for that. Skyline drive is rife with motorcyclists out to commune with nature while simultaneously blasting it with poorly muffled exhausts. This day their steady rumble shattered the peace of the woods almost continuously.

I bought dinner at Elkwallow Wayside, which saved me the time of cooking it myself but also means I'm carrying an extra meal in my food bag. During supper, I met Balls and Sunshine, a man, and his 12-year-old daughter who started April second. I'm averaging over 12 miles a day, which means they're doing over 20.

I had to hike a bit to find this campsite. I prefer established sites to avoid trampling more vegetation than necessary, but I wasn't finding something that met my fussy requirements; no soiled toilet paper lying around, a suitable food bag hang, things like that. Before I knew it, I'd covered nearly three miles more than planned. If I do the same miles tomorrow, I'll be in Front Royal for pickup shaving a day off schedule, but it will also mean pushing my leg. I guess I'll play it by ear.

—

It started raining during the night, and it never quit. I saw one hiker in the park all day. Skyline Drive was similarly deserted. There's an AT saying, "Never Quit When It's Raining"; no problem. What else is there to do but hike? It's not as if you can have a picnic or anything.

So I walked, and walked, and walked with no distractions. No views, no people, no traffic. I was perhaps a mile from the northern boundary of the Shenandoah National Park when one of the many low-lying dark shapes — that I always perceive as bears initially — did not morph into a tree stump or a rock. It remained the large pan face of a bear. Framed in forest floor greenery about four feet from the trail, I swear it looked just like the bear on the cover Bill Bryson's *A Walk in the Woods* right down to the scowl. Expecting him to move off, I approached within ten yards before stopping. He remained motionless with a fixed, inscrutable stare directed at my tasty self. I didn't want to give him time to formulate a plan while I took a picture, so I first banged my hiking poles together. With no sign of being startled or any apparent urgency, he got to his feet, and ambled about fifty yards from the trail before turning to watch as I swore at my Sony which had produced an unfocused blur. That's it for the Sony. I resumed my walk with frequent over the shoulder glances until I'd put a couple of miles between us.

I called Jan as I passed the Tom Floyd Wayside Shelter where I'd originally planned to stop. She picked me up at the next highway crossing. When we got home, I showered, had a glass of wine, ate two Boca black bean burgers, turned on the series finale of House, and fell asleep. It was 8 PM after all.

I slept well, and got up planning to do nothing much. I weighed myself. I've lost five pounds since March 2 despite eating entire pizzas, and one-pound steaks whenever I can, and carrying a food bag that thuds on a picnic table like a sack of cement. I'm now one pound under my ideal weight. I hadn't had a diet soda since I left until I drank one last night. It didn't taste as good as I remembered. I'm back to eating traditional fare, and I am trying to keep the portions reasonable.

All the walking and the damp have kept the knife wound in my foot from healing properly. Since coming home, I've gone barefoot around the house so it's gotten a chance to dry out. It looks like it's going to stay closed now. Jan bought me an insulated air mattress that weighs less than my sleeping pad. It will allow me to stay in shelters without suffering too much. It should come in handy where camping is prohibited.

Home hasn't changed much. The dog recognized me. A number of things are broken. My oldest daughter asked why nothing ever seemed to break before I left. Tomorrow I'll spend a little time fixing or replacing gear that's wearing out, but mostly I'll try to do nuthin'.

I did a lot of relaxing today, but with my return to the trail on Friday looming, we did a little preparatory shopping. My old hiking shorts were wearing out, and the waist was a little large, so we bought some new ones. They have more pockets; can't have too many pockets. I bought a Canon camera that is shorter on features than the Sony but longer on features that actually work reasonably well. I was especially impressed by its ability to stabilize the image at 20X zoom hand held. If I'd had it the other day, you'd be able to count the hairs on that bear's face. The last stop was the Wegman's supermarket, the only store I know of that carries Fantastic Foods dried refried beans, and other inexpensive, but tasty foods suitable for backpacking.

The knife wound is looking better. It will be great not feeling it with every step, and not having to worry about infection. My knee on the other hand appears to be in stasis. It bothers me even when I'm not wearing a pack, and requires manual assistance for full flexure. It will be the wild card for the remainder of this hike.

When I wake up in the middle of the night, I'm momentarily disoriented, thinking I'm still on the trail, but it passes quickly. Despite the convenience of the P jar, I much prefer walking to the bathroom provided I don't have to squirm out of a sleeping bag, and get dressed first. For a while I couldn't understand why tasks like getting dressed, and putting on my shoes is so much more difficult here, requiring that I overcome stiffness in back, and limb to accomplish it until I realized that for the last two and a half months I've been performing these tasks while lying down in the hammock. Nice to know some things will be easier when I get back to the trail.

I would like to apologize to the citizens of Stanton, er Staunton, and all the English-speaking peoples for misspelling Staunton. It's an easy mistake to make since the locals pronounce it the way I misspelled it, but that's no excuse. It was wrong, thoughtless, careless, and out of line. It won't happen again, ever, unless it does.

I called my boss Mike to say hello as I crossed from Tennessee into Virginia a little over a month ago, and he invited me to lunch with the department when I passed this way. That was today. It was great seeing everyone again. The steak wasn't so bad either. Thanks Mike, I had a great time!

I tried walking the dog without my brace this morning. We had to turn back early because I couldn't make my customary speed, and Jan had a meeting. I guess if I go lame, the time to do it is when I can call for a quick ride home.

I spent the rest of the day doing a few chores around the house, and (mostly) getting ready to get back on the trail; charging batteries, spraying more new clothes with permethrin, and fixing stuff. When Jan gets home, we'll go food shopping, and early tomorrow morning I'll rejoin the trail in Front Royal.

—

Jan dropped me off this morning, and before I knew it, I was at Jim, and Molly Denton Shelter where I stopped for lunch. I was just finishing up when CandyMan wandered out of the woods. I hadn't seen him for probably a month or more. He'd taken 7 days off to visit his American relatives in West Virginia, and got back on the trail today.

I told him I'd see him here this evening, and yadda, yadda, yadda, here I am. I was eating my dinner and thinking about where to hang my hammock when it occurred to me that I had no memory of packing it. I have no memory of many things I do so I wasn't overly concerned, but I was moved to check my pack. No hammock!

Dicks Dome Shelter is the least capacious shelter on the AT. It holds four, and it was full when I got here. I told the guys my problem. I figured the worst-case scenario was they'd say, "Gee whiz, that's a big problem for you ain't it?", and I'd walk out to a road tonight, and call Jan. As it was, they pulled their stuff toward the back of the shelter, and I put my air mattress across the opening. Then WallStreet said he'd gotten a signal up by his tent so I climbed up the hill, and called Jan. She's going to meet me with the hammock where the AT crosses US 50 tomorrow. Could have been worse I guess.

—

Jan met me at US 50 with the hammock, donuts, and a 12 pack of Pepsi. I managed the donuts, and four Pepsis. Then I hiked on to Sam Moore Shelter on a walk made arduous by heat, humidity, and The Roller Coaster, a rocky, undulating section of the AT bad enough to be worthy of its name. I passed one Boy Scout troop after another that were heading South fortunately, but when I got here, the woods were rife with scout troops out for the Memorial Day weekend.

I wouldn't call this evening magical, but it has been pleasant. There's scouts monopolizing the woods, and half a dozen through-hikers concentrated at the shelter. Some of them became concerned about a 6-foot black snake headed for the shelter. I persuaded them to leave it alone. It slithered under the shelter, and a few minutes later a mouse flew out as if it had been shot from a cannon. Later, a half hour long attempt to build a fire culminated with, "Hey, do you have any old man tricks for building a fire?" I do. Cooking with a wood stove in the past taught me to peel the bark off damp kindling. We soon had critical mass in the fire ring.

MrWrong's friend who'd come out to hike with him for the day packed in a case of beer and all the fixin's for s'mores. There were frequent trips to the stream to retrieve beer, and Hershey bars interspersed with conversation desultory, and frequently nonsensical. Good night all round.

—

I had a bad night. Intestinal upset had me doing the hundred-yard dash up hill to the privy several times. I was tired and weak when I set out in the morning. At 3.5 miles I stopped at Bear's Den Hostel, which is run by the Potomac Area Trails Club, for a shower, laundry (in the sink), and a couple of sodas. I felt much better when I left.

The first part of this section of the trail is still The Roller Coaster that has ten or eleven steep hills to climb. It isn't too bad for someone who's just hiked a thousand miles with a pack, but it was hot, and with me not completely recovered, it slowed me down, and wore me out. Fortunately, the PATC runs another hostel, The Blackburn Trail Center. It's three miles South of here, and I was ready for it. I took a quarter mile side trail to it, and bought three orange sodas. Somebody handed me an orange (the fruit) to finish up with. Then I sat on a lounge chair, and stared at the Piedmont for an hour before hiking down here to the David Lesser Shelter.

I arrived later than I typically do so I went straight to cooking without setting up the hammock. A thunderstorm came up while I was eating. I was glad the picnic table was under its own roof. Four other campers who feared dying in their tents came running up to join me. Two are snacking, one is reading a kindle, and the other is sleeping. I considered setting up the hammock under the roof here, but it looks like the storm is letting up so I'll go find a suitable site.

—

It was a long day. I hiked into Harper's Ferry, got my picture taken for registration with the Appalachian Trail Conservancy, (I'm #249 to do so this year), buy a bunch of soda, be told a guy was giving away free soda next door, meet Jan, have lunch, re-supply, and hike up here in 93 degree heat.

I did find a good place to hang my hammock last night. As I did so, the bugs came from miles around to see my headlamp. I didn't want them joining me in the hammock so I just threw in all my stuff sacks, and jumped in after them. I wasn't sure how I was going to blow up my pad inside the hammock, and get it underneath me but it I managed.

Harper's Ferry is worth a visit; beautiful old houses, great restaurants, and a downtown that's a museum of 19th century downtowns. I was glad I'd been here before when I had the time to look around because today I had miles to go before I slept. One of the hiking poles I've been using since North Carolina failed as I crossed the bridge into town. It was a locking mechanism. I had to replace it at the local outfitter who only had the generic Leki poles that everyone on the trail uses. I wrapped each one with a piece of duct tape so I could recognize mine.

I'm the only through-hiker at Ed Garvey Shelter tonight. The other guys are Peace Corps vets who did their stint in Kazakhstan and are section hiking before starting graduate school. I should take the time to single out the Peace Corps graduates I met on my hike as consistently thoughtful, engaging and kind.

It's an interesting group, but I am exhausted, and first to bed.

—

Only mad dogs and Englishmen go forth in the noonday sun.

Call me Mad Dog. This day killed ... me, but first some overdue notes on milestones. I passed out of Virginia, through West Virginia, and into Maryland. Harper's Ferry is called the psychological halfway point, but for me, the actual halfway point is the psychological halfway point. I think it's around mile 1092.

The heat and humidity sucked the life out of me today. I was worn out with half the day still in front of me. I made a quick side trip to the first monument to George Washington, and made a quick stop at Dahlgren Campground which has showers, and I took one. I didn't even bother to turn on the hot water. While I was shaving, I was amazed to see steam billowing out of a camper's shower stall.

Late in the afternoon, I was helped by a heavy thunderstorm that cooled things down quite a bit. It came up so fast I was soaked through before I could get into my rain gear. Gorp walked by me oblivious to the downpour as I was changing. It was still coming down in buckets when I got to Pine Knob Shelter. It was filled with a family outing group, but they squeezed in to give several of us a place to cook, and sit while we waited out the worst of the storm. The rain ended conveniently after dinner allowing us to set up dry shelters, and go to bed.

—

Last night I was so exhausted, and my legs ached so much that I couldn't concentrate, so I finished last night's journal entry today. It was a miserable night that included answering an emergency privy call around 1 am. I don't know what it was; heat exhaustion maybe?

It was cool this morning. I took it easy, and drank lots of water, and pink lemonade. I stopped into Ensign Cowell Shelter for a mid afternoon nap but still felt tired. I mentioned my duct-taped poles to another hiker, and he told me everybody tapes their poles. Moreover, he didn't duct tape his and someone with duct-taped poles took them by mistake anyway. When I got back on the trail, I ran into two young section hikers who asked me about my hike. As a courtesy, I asked them what their destination was.

They said, "Pen Mar."

So I said, "Oh, you're doing a loop hike then?"

"Uh Oh!" accompanied the look of shock that came over their faces. "We're going the wrong way aren't we?"

They thanked me for the information, and headed whence they came. When I got to Raven Rocks Shelter, I discovered that the spring listed in the guide as one tenth mile away was actually three tenths, a good way back down the mountain. This was especially upsetting because I'd passed up a spring on the way up based on the guide's listing.

Just after I got here, SweetTea showed up. Not a through-hiker, she is doing the Four State Challenge; hiking four states in 24 hours. She had five miles to go when she stopped here for a short rest. She wanted to lighten her load so I graciously accepted several of her homemade latte bars, and rice crispy treats. It was obvious that she was the outdoor person's outdoor person; focused, and dedicated, but what fascinated me most was that she spoke replacing her r's with w's. Vewy intewesting.

SweetTea

I was sharing the shelter with five women including a cute ridge runner (hired by the Conservancy to patrol the trail) who actually hiked in makeup. A few minutes ago, SitABit showed up.

I'm feeling much better now. I'm tempted to do a couple more miles, but I won't.

—

I slept well until the wee hours when SitABit started sawing wood like a deranged carpenter. Man he was loud. Raven Rocks Shelter has two levels, and the people upstairs started groaning, and thrashing as he buzzed away. I didn't sleep well for the rest of the night. I was afraid the malaise would return when I started hiking, but I felt good today. That was due in part to the weather. The humidity was down, and the temperature never got above 78.

MrWrong, who'd come in after SitABit, caught up with me at High Rock and took my picture for me. We hiked together briefly (he's very fast). He asked me if I thought he'd have a chance with the Potomac Area Trails Club ridge runner, the attractive young woman who'd stayed in the shelter last night. They'd talked late into the night in the vermillion glow of their headlamps so I suspected he did, but I didn't care to go in that direction so I just said, "She's very pretty, but I couldn't say."

It didn't take me long to get to Pen Mar Park. Jan, and I hiked through it two years ago on a weekend when it was alive with picnickers, and people who'd come to dance to the big band music at the pavilion. Now it was deserted. I got a soda from a machine, and sat on a bench and enjoyed the valley view. Later I learned that there is a Wal-Mart just down the street from Pen Mar. It would have been an easy re-supply.

I ran across SweetTea soaking her feet in a stream. She successfully completed her challenge, and was camped nearby with her boyfriend. I

107

reached Tumbling Run Shelters in the early afternoon. It was one of the more idyllic shelter settings, and I'd planned to stop there but it was only three more hours to Rocky Mountain Shelters, and that would give me more time to re-supply tomorrow. So I hiked on, passing the northernmost point of the AT that Jan I have hiked together. I'm back in unexplored territory.

There are only three section hikers here; a lone hiker, and a couple. The couple is getting off the trail tomorrow, and they offered me a ride into Fayetteville for my re-supply. I'm still taken by how kind and generous people can be to complete strangers.

June, 1093 Miles

I walked out with the section hikers, and they drove me into town. They gave me their names, but things not written down immediately are lost forever. Nice people though.

Fayetteville is a narrow spot on a wide road. There may be more to it, but it's too spread out to walk it. All I've seen is double wides, used car dealers, and a few other businesses strung out along US 30. The speed limit is 45, but everybody was driving much faster.

I got a room at a nearby motel. The owners, owing either to cultural differences, or to acute perception, seem to view hikers as bums. The owner didn't crack a smile, asked ten dollars more than listed in the guide, and without query, assigned me a smoking room. I couldn't help but be amused by her arrogance given that this place was likely rejected as a location for "No Country for Old Men" for being over-the-top seedy.

However, arrogance doesn't imply sophistication. There's a sign in the office welcoming reviews, and lists several hotel review sights. One red-hot review comin' up!

In contrast to the Inn is the Flamingo Restaurant. I ordered the Hog Choker breakfast. The service was great, and the meal, outstanding.

I walked a mile to the Rite-Aid, and did my re-supply there. There weren't many choices, but I got enough food to get me to Duncannon where I'll meet my friend Andy for a few days of hiking together. There's no phone directory in my room here, so I'm off to the front office to see if I can get a number for pizza delivery.

—

I was up at 5:30 and walked to the Flamingo for breakfast. I had the blueberry pancakes, and a side of ham. I'm sad to say that for the first time since Georgia, I couldn't finish. Each pancake (there were three) was half an inch thick, and covered the whole plate. When I'd whittled them down to three or so square inches, I could eat no more. I suppose it could have been the huge breakfast I'd eaten the day before, or the barbecue, coleslaw, and fries I'd eaten for lunch, or the pizza I had for supper, but there just wasn't any more room.

I left for the trail thinking I'd never need to eat again, and I didn't until lunchtime when I heated up a tub of turkey with dressing. It was cool, and the trails were mostly flat. CandyMan overtook me on a hill. He's been overtaking me since North Carolina, but he always falls behind for one reason or another.

There are two shelters here, hence the name Tom's Run Shelters. I took one for myself but later a group of some sort showed up. It's a few adults, and seven or eight kids of all races aged from about six to sixteen. I figured this had to be a disaster in the making so I said they could have the whole shelter, and I moved in with a brother sister pair (Mary & Patrick), and their two Scotties in the other shelter. The group members turned out to be unfailingly polite, even the youngest ones. They helped carry my gear over here, and thanked me for giving up my slot.

I just plan to have coffee for breakfast in the morning. The midpoint of the trail is just a few miles away, and just beyond that, the country store that sells ice cream for the Half-Gallon Challenge. I figure that can substitute for breakfast.

—

I awoke to find two stuff sacks missing. I figured those filthy stealing mice were responsible until I found them in the bottom of my pack. I made my coffee and decided a little breakfast before I moved on wouldn't hurt.

It didn't take long to reach the halfway marker, a garish wooden structure with a register. I signed in, and was about to take my picture when KitFox, and ManCub showed up, so we photographed each other.

We ran into each other again an hour later at the little store at Iron Furnace State Park, home of The Half-Gallon Challenge. ManCub and I chose Mint Chocolate Chip. KitFox got Peanut Butter Chocolate. The ice cream was hard, so I left mine on a sunny picnic table, and walked two hundred yards to the AT Museum only to discover that it wouldn't open for three hours. I returned to the table, and attacked my ice cream. The first seven eighths were delicious, but through that last eight, I was no longer at all keen about Mint Chocolate Chip and perhaps ice cream in general. I sipped coffee to offset the sweet, and finished it off. KitFox and ManCub finished their Challenge a few minutes later, and we went inside and collected our trophies: flat wooden spoons stamped with "Member of the Half-Gallon Challenge Club". Then we ate a bag of Cheetos to get the fowl taste of ice cream out of our mouths.

The Badger, KitFox and ManCub

I'd planned to eat lunch at Tagg Run Shelter, but I missed the turn-off. That's the first time I've missed a shelter I think. I wasn't very hungry anyway what with two thousand calories of Mint CC under my belt. I watered up at a country store a few miles back, and arrived here around five. It was sunny, but rain was forecast so I put up the hammock, and got my food bag rope up before I fixed dinner. Thunderclouds rolled in while I was cooking, and it poured, heavily at times, but I stayed dry under the tarp. When the time came to hoist the food bag, the branch I'd chosen snapped under the weight. It took another fifteen minutes in the rain to find a suitable hang. I got the bag up, climbed in my hammock, and fell asleep for three hours before the rain woke me up to write this entry.

—

The first item on the agenda today was a pair of rock mazes where the trail was unnecessarily routed over, and around big rocks. At some points, I had to doff my pack, throw it up ahead, and then find a way to hoist my tired old body up after it. It was a lot of fun ... lot of fun. Finally, I was happily past the mazes, and on my way to another fifteen-mile day when I came to a sign that said, "No camping between here, and Darlington Shelter". That gave me a choice between a twelve-mile day, and a twenty-two mile day. The prospect of stopping at one in the afternoon was too galling, and the trail went through Boiling Springs and gently undulating farmland so I decided to go for it.

Boiling Springs is a beautiful little town with buildings going back as far as the eighteenth century, and a spring fed lake right in the middle. I ate a pastrami sandwich at a great little deli, and took full advantage of the free soft drink refills. Then I was off.

Just to be on the safe side, I took two Aleves an hour apart and an hour after that I downed two hundred milligrams of caffeine. The miles didn't exactly melt away, but at least I felt good the whole way, even through the eight hundred foot climb at the end.

I got here at eight thirty, just as everyone else was going to bed.   There was room in the shelter so that's where I am now. I made a pot of Tuna Helper that purportedly serves four. I'm still a little hungry, but it's time to go to sleep.

—

The book said rocky trail, and unlike the time it said the spring was only 0.1 miles away, it wasn't kidding. The trail required continuous focus, and it was hard on the joints. I arrived in Duncannon in mid-afternoon, and made a beeline for the Doyle Hotel grill for lunch.

I don't know where to begin when describing the Doyle. Owned, and operated by Vicky, and Pat Kelly, this turn of the last century hotel caters to AT hikers, and frankly, I think we're the only ones who would stay here.

The only clean things in my room were the linens. There is dust, old old dust everywhere, but still, I can't help but love the place. Built in a time of varnished oak trim and transoms, the Doyle has a beauty still recognizable in its dilapidated state. My room is on the fourth floor so I asked Vicky if there was an elevator. "Sure," she answered, "right next to the concierge desk". Never did find that desk. Near as I can tell, each floor has 12 rooms, and one bathroom. There's lots of peeling paint and the roof leaks around the skylight. The rent? A very reasonable twenty-eight dollars a night.

The sparkling jewel in this tarnished crown is the Doyle Bar and Grill. Pat does the cooking, and the food is excellent. Vicky tends the bar, which doubles as the registration desk. It closes at ten PM. Unusually late for a bar that caters to hikers.

I washed my clothes in the sink down the hall, and will fall asleep to the drone of the fan, which is drying them. Tomorrow, my friend Andy who's in the adjoining room will join me for a few days.

—

Andy and I set out after breakfast. The trail was rocky at first, but smoothed out, and we had an easy hike to Pete's Mountain Shelter, arriving around 4 PM. We set up my hammock, and his tent near the shelter. The spring was down a three hundred-step rock staircase. It took me about 20 minutes to get water, and then we joined the group at the shelter to cook dinner.

The Badger and Andy

They were a genial bunch, Wonder, and Fresh, recently returned from Peace Corps stints in Peru, Dora, and Mouse, a teacher; all good conversationalists; inquisitive, knowledgeable, insightful. The first three were looking for a fourth person for Euchre, and Mouse wanted to watch to learn the game so I volunteered. I paired with Wonder. It was a good game, which we lost narrowly.

I'd first met Mouse at the Half-Gallon Challenge. That day she came across as a bubbly cheerleader; something that I'm sure endears her to most people, but which some old men can find tiresome if not insufferable. This night she was reserved, and reflective, which had me regretting my propensity for quick judgments. We chatted a bit after the game then Andy, and I departed the shelter for bed with me lamenting my slow gait. I'd likely seen Mouse, a trail rocket, for the last time.

—

Andy was surprised at how long it took us to break camp this morning. It used to surprise me too. We're used to having, and leaving every thing in its place at home. Now, as nomads, we have to pack all that we own, and carry it away on our backs.

The Pennsylvania AT is known for its rocks, and we saw our share this morning. It slowed us down quite a bit. A thunderstorm struck about a half hour before we reached our campsite in the woods, but it abated long enough for us to put up our shelters. Campers have been trickling in ever since. There's blasting going on off to the east, and large military planes are frequently seen and heard overhead.

A few days back I asked the ridge runner what the best way to dispose of toothpaste residue was if I wanted to avoid attracting fauna. She said to blow it out in a spray. As I write, a deer, not twenty feet away is meticulously licking off the leaves of the undergrowth where I sprayed my toothpaste. None of these things should keep me awake tonight.

—

We were up by 5:30 and on the trail by 7 AM. The weather was ideal for hiking, and the trail was decent too. We made it to the shuttle pickup point by mid-day. There was some miscommunication with Larry the shuttle guy, but his son eventually showed up and returned us to the Doyle for a late lunch. Then Andy drove me back to the trailhead after a quick detour to McDonald's for an early supper so I could hike more, and cook less.

This had been Andy's longest hike, and like Heinrich before him, he had suffered stoically. I'd never have known either of them was in pain were it not for the muffled sobs[1] in the middle of the night. We'd had a great time, but now we said our farewells, and parted, Andy for home, and me to my solitary Northward journey.

It started raining shortly after Andy drove off, and stopped shortly after I put my rain gear on. I remain unsure of what problem people have with hiking in the rain. It's cooler, and the rain recharges the springs. I can think of many things I'd rather not deal with, heat, mice, bears, skeeters, and snorers for example. Rain comes below hikers who debate incessantly about what constitutes a through-hike.

I'd hoped to hike the seven miles to the next shelter and was making good time despite wall-to-wall poison ivy when I hit some bodacious rock fields. My legs began to complain, and the prospect of rock scrambling in the dark with buckling knees weighed heavily. I hit some good trail, came to an old campsite after four miles, and decided to stop.

My book says it's 19.2 miles from the next shelter to the one after it so it looks like I'll be in the woods tomorrow night too. It feels like good sleeping weather. I could use a wind shift though. Right now, I'm down wind of my shoes.

—

A Tale of Two ATs

It was the best of trails; it was the worst of trails, at times flat as a pool of mercury, and surfaced in

---

[1] unverified at press time --Ed.

soft loam, at times a hellish rock pile. Judging by the time I made, it was more of the latter. I asked a hiker in the southbound lane what to expect. He said it would get rocky farther north.

It was a long day, and I was looking forward to crossing PA183 and stopping at Rentschler's Market for some ice-cold sodas. I didn't see anything when I got there. I double-checked my guide, and it said Rentschler Marker not Market. Damn my wishful thinking!

The skeeters were terrible when I got here. Even with DEET, the constant hum was distracting. I built a smoky fire. It was enough to hold them off through dinner after which I dove into my hammock, and sealed it tight. It's the first time this trip that I've been comfortable without any insulation over or under me. It does not bode well for tomorrow. Warm nights are good. Warm days I don't need.

—

Pennsylvania is The Keystone State. It's also the big stone state, the knife edged stone state, the sharp pointy stone state, and the wobbly stone state. Let's face it. It's one big stoned state, and it's tearing up my shoes, my knees, and my feet. It was also hot, and humid. I arrived at the Port Clinton Hotel with empty water bottles.

Like the Doyle, this hotel has no AC, and the bathroom is down the hall. Like the Doyle, the bar, and restaurant are excellent. I had a steak served with actual vegetables. Unlike the Doyle, the room seems to have been dusted in the not too distant past, and it has TV although I haven't had time to watch. They also charge twice as much for a room. Cleanliness and meager entertainment has a price.

I resupplied at the Wal-Mart. It's a mile and a half down a busy highway, and I had no luck hitching. My efforts in that regard were half-baked because the traffic was so heavy and fast I was afraid someone stopping would precipitate a chain reaction accident. I got back just as the restaurant closed so I missed my second supper. I just finished getting everything staged for tomorrow. It's eleven thirty, way too late to be up writing.

—

I was up at five. That proved to be a foolish mistake. I was tired all day. The hotel doesn't serve breakfast, which is kinda weird I think. I walked a mile up the highway to the village of Molino where the only visible structure is the 3C's Restaurant. I had their special plus a piece of apple pie.

Then it was back to Port Clinton, and its three extant businesses, the hotel, a candy store, and a motorcycle dealership. Incorporated in 1850, it was likely a pleasant community later ruined when the highway evolved into a high-speed artery of commerce.

Back on the trail on the climb out of town, I ran into Dropout, a young man who took a year off from college to hike. I'd met him in the Wal-Mart the night before. He is unique in that he doesn't cook which makes for some interesting food choices. He eats things like canned chicken salad, saltines with peanut butter — I could get into that myself — and fruit cups. We walked together until noon, which came up quickly. A good trail conversation will do that.

This place, Elkville Shelter, is a luxury operation. It has a flush toilet, and a solar shower. A restaurant delivers from a few miles away. It's run by a live-in caretaker who can be a cantankerous SOB, but one who has been known to go out of his way to be helpful at times, and is capable of generous acts. He interceded with the restaurant for a food delivery problem so we ordered extra coke, and gave him some. Then, when he noticed I have a computer, he volunteered that he had Wi-Fi, something both unadvertised and unexpected. Just a few minutes ago, he brought us frozen cool-pops, a most welcome treat.

The group tonight is docile, made so by large infusions of pizza, and soda. I don't know most of them except for Duffer (whom I've leapfrogged with since Watauga Lake) and Maniac. I met her at Loft Mountain in the Shenandoah Park. Both have taken numerous days off since.

—

Okay, I can think of one time when rain moves up my list of bothersome things on the trail. I have to admit it would be a little bit nicer to cross a knife edged ridge composed of giant jumbled rocks if I didn't have to worry about slipping on a wet rock and falling to my death.

Duffer wanted to hike with me today and I'm glad he did. We hit it off pretty well. He's a retired EPA lawyer and had some interesting stories to tell. It started raining shortly after we hit the trail, and fourteen hours later, it is still coming down. We hit rock field after rock field. The longest took more than an hour to cross, but it wasn't the worst. The knife edged ridge took intense concentration on every aspect of movement from foot and pole placement to making sure my center of gravity was always situated so that slipping wouldn't result in a fall over the edge. Once past it, we made good time until we hit one last field of huge rocks, and bad potential falls before reaching Bake Oven Knob Shelter, which is a tiny hole in the wall, but a dry one.

After a hot dinner, I found water in my pack for the first time ever. I can't figure out how it got in. I had it covered by my jacket or my tarp all day. It wasn't much but it was enough to get the foot end of my sleeping bag wet. Fortunately, the silk liner stayed dry, and I don't need much more than that to stay warm tonight. I have a trash bag I can put the sleeping bag in tomorrow if it's still raining. We agreed that overall, this was our most intense day on the trail ever.

—

No one else came to the shelter last night, which was a relief. We'd spread out wet gear everywhere. We made slow progress most of the day owing to those confounded rocks. It was a little easier going today because the sun was out and drying the trails off. When we stopped for lunch we spread our gear out on the grass, and I managed to dry everything except my shoes and socks, which smell like a wet dog with lower tract issues.

Then it was on to The Climb of Death. I had an inkling things might be going south when we encountered a copperhead sunning himself on the trail. He wouldn't move out of the way even after we tossed sand and rocks his way. Eventually he slithered off the trail when I nudged him with a hiking pole. Not long after that, we found ourselves climbing ever steeper rock formations. The only evidence of a trail was the blazes. We negotiated six-inch ledges using cracks in the wall for handholds. I was both afraid, and angry that we had to make such an unsafe traverse.

Duffer said he was glad he wasn't alone on this part of the trail. I said, "Me too" but thought that had I been alone, I could have hired a limo to take me to New Jersey, and no one would have been the wiser.

We didn't make our mileage goal today owing to poor to unsafe trail conditions, but we made it far enough to be able to walk into Wind Gap tomorrow for re-supply.

When we arrived here, I found two ticks on my leg. Neither was embedded yet. Nor had either one made it under my permethrined clothing. Lucky ticks.

—

Billy wandered into our campsite after supper last night and set up his tent. He asked if he could hang his food on our rope, which was fine with us. He also asked us to wake him when we got up at five, which was also fine, but his good intentions had evaporated when I called on his tent this morning, and he was soon sound asleep again.

The trail wasn't particularly bad or good, but there were none of the infernal rock obstacles we'd encountered the last couple of days so we made a little better than 2mph. When I sat down for lunch, I noticed the tops of my Salomon trail runners were beginning to disintegrate.

About then, MrWrong loped up. After hearing about my problem, he suggested I call Salomon, which I did. Apparently, many manufacturers that serve the backpacking sport are especially helpful to AT hikers because they aren't in a position to seek help elsewhere. Salomon was out of stock indefinitely. They suggested I go back to Zappo's where I'd made my purchase. I didn't see what skin they had in this game, but to my surprise, they gave me a courtesy replacement, which they will overnight to a motel in Delaware Water Gap. Since I was on a roll, I called Osprey, and told them about the holes that had started growing in the trampoline frame netting of my pack. Osprey is going to send me a new pack free including shipping.

Duffer continues to be excellent company. The miles have fallen away as we recount our life experience. We've agreed to hike on together, and share room expenses for a week or two at least. It's going to take some adjustment. He is a planner, and I'm not. He maps out where he'll be weeks ahead of time, and bounces a box from post office to post office from which he can retrieve various items when he needs them. Meanwhile, his wife puts together meal requests, and mails them to him. Even if I could plan that far in advance, I couldn't remember it, and if I wrote it down, I'd forget where I put it. No matter, it looks like it'll be fun. We're in Wind Gap, Pennsylvania.

—

We're almost out of Rocksylvania! We had some good hiking on old roads, but mostly it was on feet chewing rocks or gigantic climbing rocks. We made it to Delaware Water Gap, a leafy community only three tenths of a mile from the New Jersey border. South bounders have told us that the worst is over.

Not a moment too soon. I have inflamed feet, and shooting pains in my left leg. My new shoes were waiting for me at the Pocono Inn. I need to ship the old ones back to get credit, and that's looking difficult. The desk clerk said he couldn't print out the shipping label. He had one computer with a printer but no Internet, and one with Internet but no printer. He said, "Can't be done. I'd have to move this cable from that computer to this one you see". The welcome center might do it but it won't open until ten. I'll have to see what I can beg from the outfitter. We met the outfitter earlier as he was locking his front door and asked him when he'd be open today. "Nine or ten" he said. I'm getting the impression that the prevalent business model around here assumes that things go much more smoothly if you don't have to put up with customers, and their nettlesome queries.

It's paradoxical that people who must sell services for their livelihood are so disinterested, while so many others who need nothing from us give so much without compensation. Anyway, we'll be at the outfitters at nine or ten sharp to see what he can do for me.

The post office doesn't open until nine any way, so it doesn't look like big miles tomorrow. Gee whiz, too bad. I'm going to try to get a good night's rest and hope that de feets, and de legs get better by tomorrow.

—

We were up at 5 AM and off to the Diner for a delicious breakfast and then to an outfitter who opened before ten where I inquired as to whether she would mind printing my Zappos shipping label. It took her less than a minute. We got everything shipped, and headed out of town. Duffer stopped for a haircut on the way.

Then it was across the Delaware River Bridge and into New Jersey. I looked back at Pennsylvania from atop the bluff, shook a bitter fist at the rocks on the Pennsylvania AT and turned my back on them forever.

The trails were better here but not a lot better. I'm told the geology doesn't change until we cross the Hudson. We made reasonable miles considering that we left so late. We ate an hour before arriving at this campsite at Rattlesnake Spring Campground to confound the bears. Bears are protected in NJ so their fear of humans is attenuated. After we got here, lots of people started showing up and began cooking dinner. So much for cooking far away.

—

Some time this morning, during a break I think, I realized that our low miles would result in our arrival at my next re-supply point after my food has run out. To remedy this we needed to rack up about 18 miles today. That isn't very difficult unless you happen to have a leg that reminds you whenever it is being taxed, and a bad case of localized dermatitis[1].

While we were on a break, and I was off attending to some important off trail business, Duffer heard what sounded like a hiker coming up the trail. When he turned to look, he saw two big round black ears bobbing above the grass. He clapped his hands, and up popped a bear's head. As we know, bears are shameless cravens, so as soon as he saw Duffer, he bolted. I'm glad Duffer was there. I wouldn't want to be caught alone with my pants down.

---

[1] Monkey butt

We didn't do particularly well mile wise until our speed started picking up in mid-afternoon. Perhaps we were inspired by the revelation that there is a restaurant just off the trail where the AT crosses US230. We decided to stop there for a morale boost and because eating there would make my trail food last longer.

I had a great restaurant meal at Stoke's Steakhouse where we joined up with TenYear, a section hiker who plans to finish the whole AT in ten years, for the walk up to Gren Anderson Shelter. The three of us had a good talk, and before we knew it, we were in camp. Nice place. It has the first bear box I've seen in the east, and the spring is a short walk away. The Euchre players Wonder and Fresh are here, but I've had a couple of beers, and am ready for bed.

—

The AT is designated a National Scenic Trail. As I walked this morning, I had to keep my eyes glued to the ground to negotiate the ankle twisters and shoe shredders. For all I know the trail was lined with bald eagles in tutus saluting as we passed. So my question to you is, if you can't look at anything without endangering yourself or your property, is it a scenic trail?

We began to focus on a late lunch at the concession at Highpoint State Park beach to take our mind of our troubles. Conditions were so bad; we didn't get to the turn off until about 2:30. The side trail came to a road where we found no signs or blazes to tell us which way to turn.

A passerby with a poor command of English whom I'll call Schneckelholfer told us to go right. I said, "I dunno guys, I hear beach sounds coming from the left" to which TenYear replied, "The road probably doubles back. I bushwhacked about ten yards off the road toward the lake, and it looked like the woods went all the way down to the water. TenYear said I probably didn't go down far enough, and besides, why would Schneckelholfer lie to us? It occurred to me that he may have misunderstood the question, or simply was venting contempt for Americans, but he was well down the road so there was no quizzing him now. We went right. When we got to the end of the lake, we could see the beach and concession all the way at the other end.

We spotted a wide gravel path along the lake edge so we figured that at least we didn't have to retrace our steps back up the hill. The path ended about half way around the lake leaving us to bushwhack over rocks, and through scratchy bushes. We finished our "lunch" of hotdogs, sodas, and ice cream at 4:00, and were back on the trail.

Not long after that, we caught our first big break of the day. The trail came off the stony ridges, and descended to soft New Jersey bottomland. We made great time to the Murray Property, which has a shower on the side of an outbuilding with no curtain so everyone can judge your physical attributes as you wash. There's a large lawn for tenting and a small bunkhouse that locks so we can store our food away from bears. It also has outlets and a fan. I washed my clothes at the shower and hung them to dry in front of the fan. It's comfortable in there so I'm going to sleep on the floor instead of in my hammock so I can get away early to Unionville for re-supply. I left my toilet paper, and hand sanitizer in the privy at Gren Anderson; more stuff to buy.

—

Our next scheduled stop after Murray was Unionville, NY for breakfast. When we reached the road the book called out, Duffer, and TenYear didn't think it was the right one so we consulted with Schneckelholfer who happened by as we reached the road. It wasn't really the same guy as yesterday. He said the name of the road was Quarry Road in American English. We were looking for Lott Road so we moved on. No more roads were showing up, and the time was telling us we should have been there so I consulted my GPS.

I don't know why I hadn't done so sooner or at the lake yesterday for that matter. The GPS said the road we'd crossed was Lott Rd. When Duffer came up, I gave him the bad news, and he said, "That must be wrong! We have Schneckelhofer's word!". He said these mean and hurtful words within earshot of my poor GPS! The GPS turned out to be right. We lost about a half hour to the bogus directions.

Whoever said trail conditions don't get better before we cross the Hudson was wrong. We've had decent trails and are making good progress. Duffer, and I have been pushing it to get into Greenwood Lake early enough to give us a near zero day to relax a little bit before my friend Daniel arrives to hike with us on Friday. I seem to have miscalculated. We get into Greenwood tomorrow, which gives us half of Wednesday, and all of Thursday off! I've had worse things happen to me on this trail.

—

Today's hiking was as arduous as yesterday's was easy. It was over 90, and there were major rock scrambles. We finished the ten miles into

Greenwood around one thirty but I felt like we'd done twenty.

We took a cab from the road crossing to the Breezy Inn and Motel where we had excellent food in bird size portions. My new pack was here. I had to empty my old pack to send back, and was surprised at how much came out of it. We took another cab from the motel to the post office after which we split up. Me to re-supply, and Duffer to the Motel to plan his next leg. Duffer decided not to zero here after all, but rather to do it at the end of the month to synchronize with meeting his wife.

Truth be told, Duffer is a long-range planner, and a consistently fast hiker. I am neither, going fast when I concentrate, and slowing down when lost in thought. I think that stressed both of us at times. All in all, it was a positive experience, and we may get back together to hike the White Mountains later on. So tomorrow, we part. Duffer to hike on, me to rest up, await Daniel's arrival, and begin "The Race to the Hudson".

—

Don't go out in the woods today ... for if you go out in the woods today you may see someone hiking naked. Summer Solstice is Hike Naked Day. Owing to the alignment of the sun, and the earth, and other odds, and ends, it is permissible to hike without your clothes on June 21st. It is a concept that men grasp intuitively, but one which a few women get even after in-depth explanations accompanied with detailed diagrams, and equations. In any event, I'm happy to be sweltering on the veranda with nothing but an ice-cold margarita to console me.

After Duffer and I said our goodbyes, I walked to town for breakfast this morning. Greenwood is a compact little town that serves the resort community around Greenwood Lake, or Long Pond. The former being what most of us native Americans call it, the latter being the name the aboriginal native Americans gave it back in the day.

I stopped on the way at the hardware store to inquire after stove fuel by the ounce. The proprietor smiled, and said, "Don't sell it that way." However, he would happily sell me a quantity that would, with judicious husbandry, see me well past the North Pole. Now I do understand that selling fuel by the ounce can be pain even at the usual six or seven-hundred percent markup, but here is where I got confused.

He said a couple of hikers bought a big can of fuel last year, extracted as much as they wanted to carry on their backs, and left the rest requesting that the owner dispense the remainder for free to other hikers which he happily did for a couple of months! Once again, I leave it to the social scientists out there to unravel this inconsistent behavior. My theory is that he's a knucklehead.

I received some unhappy news from Hoot's girlfriend this evening. Hoot, whom I last saw disappearing into the rain at route 60 in Virginia, was diagnosed with Lyme disease. He left the trail at Rt. 52 in NY, and is recovering at his home. It's too early to tell whether he'll get back on the trail this year.[1]

---

[1] Turns out he didn't, but I'm happy to say that after many injuries, and various other interruptions, he finished in 2017.

Daniel didn't get in until after midnight because his first ride never showed. It wasn't a big problem because the cab company here that took us to the trail doesn't open until nine AM giving us plenty of time to sleep in. We walked into town for breakfast. Then we caught a cab back to the trail.

It was sweltering, and trail conditions were not good. Progress was slow. This afternoon we came across several gallon jugs of water that had been left for hikers at the trailhead. It was welcome because there are few good springs hereabouts.

A couple of thunderstorms came through in the afternoon. We were glad we'd passed most of the bad sections of trail when it started raining, but there were still a few slippery rocky areas ahead. The storm did cool the air making hiking a little faster. We cooked dinner around six, and then walked for another hour to Island Pond where we are being serenaded by bullfrogs.

—

I fell asleep before I could write a word this evening. When I awoke an hour later, I was cold. I donned a long sleeve shirt. That effort had me wide-awake and ready to write. It was slow going again today owing to washboard terrain and obstacles such as The Lemon Squeezer, which had us doffing our packs to negotiate a narrow slot in the rocks. We topped Black Mountain where my guidebook said we could expect to see New York City. I looked down the Hudson but saw nothing, then off to the right I spied the skyline of Manhattan. I'm still searching for the words to properly describe the majestic gray on blue outline that appeared to be floating above the horizon.

Daniel and The Badger

We were on the trail by six forty but had made only about 14 miles by six PM when we decided to stop for the day. We should be over this mountain and in the park in an hour or two tomorrow morning. There Daniel will collect his car and I will hook up with my younger sister, my niece, and nephew.

I've enjoyed hiking with Daniel. His youthful perspective is very different from mine, and it's been fun discussing various and sundry topics as we hiked. He's a mountaineer, and in excellent shape which makes him capable of hiking much faster than I hike. That said, he's been patient and good humored as I've struggled to make headway. Tomorrow night I'll be alone again, preparing for the final 800 miles and wondering what adventures they'll serve up.

—

If the entire AT was like the carefully manicured specimens on the slopes of Bear Mountain, I'd be sipping a celebratory margarita on the summit of Katahdin right now. Volunteers are removing some trails, and revamping others on Bear Mountain, and they are doing a fantastic job.

We had an interesting evening. Daniel had no insulating pad in his hammock. I thought maybe it was warm enough to forego one myself, but by midnight, I was sleeping comfortably atop my air mattress. There was little Daniel could do but put on all the clothes he had, and hope for the best. He got cold, but survived the night.

When I woke up, I was thirsty so I did the pinch test, and discovered I was dehydrated. I drank all my remaining water. When we summited Bear Mountain, I bought Gatorade from a machine near the lookout tower. Once we were off the mountain, I drank as much as I could, and am in pretty good shape now.

We checked out the attractions in the park between the mountain, and the Hudson. We ran into the JerseyBoys, whom I'd last seen marching past me in lockstep back in North Carolina. I'd fully expected that they'd have finished the AT by now, but they've been stopping to smell the roses. Daniel departed after my Manhattan relatives arrived. We spent the afternoon in conversation over a few beers followed by a good dinner. They're safely back in the city now. It's been a good day.

—

I awoke to a forecast of a one hundred percent chance of rain. That proved correct right after breakfast. It rained hard for a short while then it let up while the owner of the Motel drove me down to the trail. There was another deluge covering my climb up the bluff on the other side of the Hudson River.

Around lunchtime, I came out of the woods at a highway intersection, and there right in front of me was a gas station and 24 hour deli. Now see, that's something we need more of. I had a slice of cheese Pizza, and a can of Pepsi, and was energized for the rest of the afternoon. Sometime after that, a young female section hiker who said she was working on her undergraduate anthropology thesis overtook me. She was compiling reasons given for why people hike the trail. We talked for a couple of hours while we hiked. Her informal conversation was full of likes, and awesomes, but when she spoke of her work, she articulated like an academic. It was an interesting conversation.

We split up at a water source, and I continued to my campsite in the woods. There was one more downpour while I was eating dinner sitting in my hammock under the tarp. I stayed pretty dry the entire day. That's about it. All that remains is to thumb my nose at the blood sucking skeeter horde hovering about my bug net and turn out the lights.

—

When I was hiking with Duffer, he mentioned coming around a corner, and encountering MamawB[1] naked from the waist up, washing in a stream. I had no idea who MamawB was, but when I met her and her two hiking companions today, I recognized the woman I'd hiked with for half a day back in Georgia who had no trail name at the time, and who I hadn't seen since. Small world.

---

[1] At 74, MamawB was the oldest woman ever to hike the AT, and a fine physical specimen.

I hiked big miles today mainly because I subtracted wrong and thought I needed to get here to put in 15 miles. The weather was perfect for it and the trail conditions good for the most part. I arrived at the Taconic underpass at noon and encountered BlisterQueen handing out trail magic from her car. What magic it was! New York bagels, smoked salmon, Vidalia onions, sliced tomatoes, and creamed cheese. My sister brings these delicacies family gatherings where I, because I count calories, apply the toppings to my bagel sparingly. There was no such silliness today. I piled it on high, and deep. I also had some sodas, a beer, several slices of watermelon, and a peanut butter sandwich.

I got to Morgan Stewart Shelter around six. Everyone else rolled in late because they hiked a third of a mile off trail to go to a deli. For once, I didn't feel the need. The anthropologist is here, MamawB, and her friends, and TenYear who is now hiking with his wife and daughter[1] for a week. I'm sleeping in the shelter tonight so I can make a quick break for Pawling NY for re-supply.

—

I was a little slow getting out of the shelter but a good trail had me on track to get into Pawling in plenty of time to pick up my package and re-supply, and possibly even put in some more miles after Pawling. I was about an hour out when I stumbled on a rock, and my free pole caught on a root. It was an extremely unfortunate confluence of events. I was going to crash. I made a five-point landing on my knees hands, and face. The face part shocks

---

[1] Later I heard TenYear and his wife divorced, and his daughter hiked the AT the next year.

hikers when it happens for the first time. It's the inertia of the pack. There's no stopping it as it carries your face with it into the dirt. Hikers who react quickly can avoid this indignity by flipping over and landing on their packs, but rarely do I manage it.

I delivered a torrent of curses to everything remotely connected to this incident before attending to the damage. I washed my face, and hands, and rinsed the cuts on my right knee. (This knee had an expensive Futuro brace with a patella hole that left the kneecap unprotected. The other knee had a cheap two-buck Wal-Mart brace and was unscathed). I wound things up with some Nu-skin on the cuts just as the women, MamawB, Rainbow, and NutterButter hiked past. I was hurting big time, but as I now looked great, and was required to display stoicism per the Man Code, I was denied an opportunity for a get-well candy bar or even for a little feminine sympathy.

It was a trying moment, the kind of moment that calls for pie, so I sat down, and ate a piece. Once I'd limped to the road, I hitched a ride into Pawling, which is a minor miracle in itself considering hitching is outlawed in New York. I ate a pizza for lunch, re-supplied at the local CVS because the supermarket was 3 miles out of town. There wasn't a lot of choice. I'll be eating Pop Tarts for another four days. There was no package at the post office so I called Jan to ream her out for shameful foot dragging. Turned out I told her to send the package to my next stop up the trail. Fortunately, we figured this out before I had a chance to heat up the rhetoric.

The town provides a free campsite for hikers at Edward R. Morrow Memorial Park pavilion. I'm alone which is a little creepy given the heavy vandalism and a bear, which recently nosed about town for a couple of days. On the up side, it has an outlet at which I re-charged my phone. An older man stopped by with his dogs, and asked me if there was anything I needed. The pavilion is about 5 miles from the trailhead so I said a ride would be nice. He seemed to blanch at getting up at an early hour so I offered to buy him breakfast at the Quick Stop. The worst that can happen is I'll end up walking five miles that don't count tomorrow; at least I hope that's the worst.

—

I left New York behind me today and am in Connecticut now. This is also the day that I received a flurry of emails letting me know that the Supreme Court upheld Obamacare.

Around ten thirty last night, I heard voices approaching. I thought they might be hikers so I turned on my headlamp and asked. A startled girl said, "No! Who the hell are you?" I said I was a hiker, and the village was letting me camp in the pavilion. They talked amongst themselves, and departed. I didn't sleep very well after that.

I got up this morning to discover that owing to yesterday's crash landing, one leg was paralyzed, and I couldn't move the other, but through some sort of synergistic coupling between the two, I managed to waddle like the plastic duck with swingy feet that I had as a child. The duck was much faster than I was of course, but you get the idea.

I tottered on down to the Quick Stop, and called Steve, the guy I'd met at the Pavilion the night before. He came right down, refused my offer of breakfast, chatted while I ate, and drove me back to the trailhead. He was more interesting than I first surmised. He'd been an activist, and a social worker.

My legs loosened up as the day progressed, and by this afternoon I was walking pretty normally so I poured on the miles, and ended up at Schaghticoke Connecticut Campsite with all new people including Trog who's making his third attempt at completing the AT. He's been knocked off by illness in past years, but has always come back, and finished the parts he missed. But that's not good enough for him. Good enough for me though. This year he's hiking with OldGoose and DreamTime.

—

I hiked from 7 AM to 8 at night with time off for lunch, and supper. Fifteen miles is all it got me, and it took me until three thirty to get ten of those. The trails were poor this morning, it was hot this afternoon, and I felt weak and lightheaded during most of the day. I might also have a blister under the arch of a middle toe. I feel a lump there, but whenever I try to look, my leg cramps up.

The descent to the Housatonic River was dangerous. The book called them steep stone steps, but it was more like jagged rocks with drop-offs of death. The only reason I made it this far was that the walk along the Housatonic was very flat, and I made back a lot of time.

Other fun stuff included a 0.2-mile walk on a side trail to a water pump that didn't work, and a creek that I had to ford to avoid an alternate trail that would have added more distance to hike. I arrived at this patch in the woods at dusk. Serious skeeters here. I'm grateful to whoever invented DEET.

I'm still on track to make it to Salisbury midday Sunday.

—

It was another scorcher. Things started poorly and stayed that way. I was continually being called off the trail to transact important business. To put it bluntly, it was not a day on which I could risk farting with my pants on. I'd made about five miles by lunchtime.

I was sitting on a rock cooking when OldGoose and DreamTime came up, and stopped long enough to hear of my troubles. DreamTime's husband Andy was picking them, and Trog up at route 7, and DreamTime invited me to join them.

Trog came along after they left and hiked with me. He was a little faster than I was especially since his pack only had a lunch, and a few odds, and ends in it, but I could keep up. When we reached Andy's car, I was served a Gatorade and a beer after which we went out to eat. All of these things improved my sense of well being immensely. Tomorrow we'll have breakfast here — we're staying at Maria McCabe's Hostel in Salisbury — then Andy will drop us off at route 7 with packs containing only food and water (this is called slack packing), and we'll hike back here. Sweet! Especially DreamTime and Andy, two very thoughtful and generous people.

July, 1511 Miles

So this is what pain free hiking is like. We left for the trail after an unhurried breakfast during which OldGoose stole Trog's plate when he was distracted, an infraction, which went unnoticed by the victim. We were soon engaged in the most effortless hike I've experienced since I started in March. With my burden reduced to under ten pounds — I was carrying water, a sandwich, and rain gear — my knees complained only on the really steep parts of the trail, and there were very few of those. I covered almost eleven miles in four hours!

Granted the trail conditions were the best in recent memory, mostly soft pine needles interspersed with hay fields. Even so, I could never have hiked so fast nor kept up with the others for the most part had I been carrying a full load. The experience has me re-evaluating my gear to see what can be pared. I'll likely send the bear repellant home. It's heavy, no one else carries it, and my only bear encounter didn't require its use.

Tomorrow it's off to the hospital in Sharon to make sure I'm not suffering from any infections, particularly ones that might be exacerbated by strenuous exercise, and then it's on to Massachusetts.

—

I am now a couple of miles inside Massachusetts. Maria McCabe is a twice-widowed 83-year-old woman who takes in hikers to make a little walking around money, too little in my opinion. For thirty-five dollars, she gives you a bed with clean sheets, a shower, and breakfast. She supplies eggs, juice coffee, bananas, and muffins. The guests do the preparation because Maria doesn't get out of bed before nine. This morning I made the coffee, and Andy cooked the eggs.

Andy drove me to the hospital in Sharon after breakfast. The drive was a treat in itself. The road is dotted with quaint little towns with tree-lined streets and well-maintained buildings. The merchants have learned to do without garish signage. They've also learned that customers enjoy shaded parking lots with the same fervor with which they abhor hot asphalt deserts.

At the emergency room, they took blood and samples from most every orifice and told me they'd get back to me in three to four days. Marie drove down and took me to the post office to pick up my package and then to her house. She has a thick German accent so I hit her up with a "Sie sind Deutch?" which amused her. She refused compensation for driving down to Sharon so I pretended not to have correct change when I paid my bill for two days lodging. She finally agreed to accept the surplus as gas money.

So once again, people who were complete strangers a day or two before had treated me like a favorite relative. Not only were they kind, and generous with their time, and resources, they were pleasant company with whom I enjoyed passing the time. It was hugs and handshakes all around when I departed for the hospital, and a big hug for Maria when she dropped me off at the trail this afternoon.

The trail was good going up Bear Mountain, the highest peak in Connecticut. The humidity was low, the temperature was in the seventies, and a breeze kept the moskwitos at bay making the hike more like a walk in the woods, and   less like skirting Hell's maw.

I toyed with the idea of catching up with DreamTime, Trog, and   OldGoose but scotched it when the descent from Bear proved a bear. This is an actual official campsite with privy, bear proof food box, and several elevated tent pads. I'm the lone inhabitant tonight though. I received a voice mail from Trog asking how I was when I turned my phone on for a position check. It's time to send him a text.

—

My hammock was aligned East West so I got to watch the sunrise while I greased my toes with A&D ointment this morning. I wasn't alone after all. The NoodleHeads walked past me as I was enjoying my morning coffee. They'd camped on a little flat spot just below me. It was in the sixties and seventies this morning but the trail was ups and downs over steeply slanted rock that looked like lava flows.

I was atop Mount Everett when I met a shirtless man wearing a daypack. He said he was out doing some trail magic. I asked him what he planned to give away and   he said he had trail food, water, and   toilet paper; three things that of which virtually every hiker has enough. He had a strange affect, and   spoke in monotone. He followed me for a while, and   eventually said he was starting an alcohol stove business and   wanted to make videos of hikers using his product. I said I didn't have a lot of time but I'd do a four-minute video if he'd top off my water. He took off for a parking lot where he had his video equipment and   where I caught up with him a half hour later.

He placed a stove on the ground in front of me, put a pot of water on it and   commenced recording the process. He didn't ask me to do anything. He talked about this and that as he recorded, and came over once to adjust the cooking setup. It was either a sophisticated attempt to make a through-hiker look silly or a pathetic business venture. He gave me some ice water for my trouble. I said if he had difficulty getting participants, he might try offering cold Pepsi. He said he didn't have any. I decided there was no helping this guy, and said my farewell.

I was making dismal mileage and   wondering if it was disease, age or ill-conceived trail design. Whatever it was, it was depressing. By two PM, I'd had enough. I found a bed of pine needles, took an Aleve and some caffeine, and   lay down, and   went to sleep. When the caffeine woke me half an hour later, most of my pain was gone, and   I felt better physically at least.

I started down Mount Bushnell, and   soon came to something I'd often wondered about, but never heard of or seen. The blazes turned abruptly and led off a cliff. This wasn't entirely inconsistent with other features I'd encountered in the morning so it took some reconnoitering to convince myself the blazes were in fact a prank, and   the real trail proceeded down a gentler slope.

I encountered flat soft trails about an hour later and   began making miles. Being in the lowlands now, I opted not to draw ag runoff for drinking. A kindly old woman living in a cottage at the edge of the forest filled my bottles from her sink. She fretted that she'd be in big trouble if her daughter were to find out she'd opened her door to a stranger.

Not long after that, I came across a cooler full of sodas. A couple of guys were there ahead of me. One of them, Spider, I'd met in Tennessee the night before I got to Uncle Johnnies, and not seen again until now. Averaged out, it turned out to be a good day.

—

Happy Fourth of July!! It rained last night, and it was hot this morning making hiking in the woods about as much fun as stacking bags of manure in a greenhouse. The trails weren't too bad though so by lunch time I'd come six miles.

Rather than eat in some dank hollow, I settled for a trailhead parking area. I setup with a map kiosk support as my backrest and ate. I was finishing up when a young woman drove up with her toddler. She asked if I was hiking the AT, and when I said I was, she offered me all sorts of things, the most welcome of which was some Gatorade. It was clearly ad hoc, but welcome nonetheless. I got her name but neglected to write it down right away so, you know.

I guess I'll have to take back what I said about water not being particularly welcome trail magic. Usually it's not, but we're in a bit of a drought. Many water sources have dried up. All that remains of the water here at Mount Wilcox North Shelter, listed as a reliable water source, is a tiny puddle. I've downed at least a gallon today including the two small bottles of Gatorade the nice lady gave me

145

plus two 20 oz Gatorade powders, and   I'm still thirsty. I have about a liter left for breakfast.

I cut my miles to twelve today to get a little rest, but mostly so I could stay at a shelter and   have some company for a change. So far, it looks like this will be the first time I've stayed at a shelter with nothing but bugs for company if the bugs come back.

I built a smoldering fire as soon as I got here that lasted for several hours, and   swept the area clean of insects. It looks like I'll get to bed early, and   get a good night's sleep. Tomorrow I'll contact the hospital for my test results.

—

I could hear fireworks from several directions in the evening, but couldn't see any. The skeeters came back after I'd gone to sleep, and   made enough noise to wake me up. I had 100 percent DEET on, and   a bug net over my face, but the collective hum of the cloud of unholy bloodsuckers was so disconcerting, I could only sleep in fits, and starts.

I got up earlier than usual, and   bolted for the trail. It wasn't long before I ran into the GourmetGirls slack packing in the opposite direction. I hadn't seen them since before Waynesboro. They said Duffer was just a mile ahead, but he was planning on big miles. I planned on ten miles, but someone on the trail said they serve a pancake breakfast at Upper Goose Pond Cabin so I thought what the heck. Only two miles more, and a donation, and I won't have to cook.

The local trail club runs this cabin. Volunteer caretakers rotate out by the week. There are bunks for over 15 people, and more can camp. I'd say there are about ten hikers tonight. There's a lake for swimming, and canoeing, but I didn't have time for that. There's a place for washing up so I did a quick sponge bath and feel a lot better for it. The caretaker let me use the gas stove which saved me a little fuel, and made supper more convenient.

The NoodleHeads are here. They're a youngish couple from Colorado. Neither of them works, per se. They do things like housesitting to keep costs at a minimum, and hike a lot. They seem to enjoy the lifestyle.

The hospital said all my tests came back negative. The only new thing they found was an indistinct heart murmur which was characterized as "nothing to worry about". I don't know what my problem was, maybe heat exhaustion. So, I'm doomed to hike on.

Nomad, a section hiker from Pittsfield brought a cold six-pack of Bud with him, but he could only finish four. Gee whizz, what a shame. What to do. What to do.

—

This morning I noticed that my right kneecap was twice the size of the left, and the flesh had taken on the consistency of pizza dough. It's not painful though, so I'm a walkin' with it. Knowing I didn't have to make big miles to make my rendezvous with my neighbor's brother Andy, I ate a leisurely pancake breakfast at the cabin, and conversed with a few guests. Having no confidence that I'd find good water on the trail, I drank until I could drink no more. Then I topped off my bottles before departing.

The trail wasn't too harsh, but there were many rooty rocky areas, lots of ten, twenty-foot ups, and downs. I was right about the water. When my first bottle was empty, there was only water from a slow stream to refill with. When I reached the parking lot where I was going to meet Andy I found a shady spot, sat down, and read my AT Guide to take my mind off the greenish effluent I'd be cooking with this evening.

The first thing that caught my eye was an entry about a woman who makes cookies, and gives water to AT hikers. She lives about 100 yards from where I was sitting. I was on my feet and down the road in an instant. When I got to her house, I found placards noting that she also sold soft drinks, ice cream bars, farm fresh eggs, and allowed camping in her yard. I gotta pay more attention to the AT Guide entries.

I called Andy, and let him know our meeting place had shifted. The couple that lives here are elderly and very generous. They serve everyone homemade cookies and sell everything else at a price best characterized as nominal. There's even a flush toilet for us in an outbuilding. You have to use a bucket to flush it, and refill it for the next user, but I don't mind. T and FivePair don't seem to be too eager to use it though.

Other hikers came and went. I ate dinner. Andy showed up with two 16 oz. bottles of Pepsi packed in ice, just as he'd promised. Good old Andy. We ordered up nine boiled eggs for breakfast. It should be a good hike into Dalton tomorrow.

—

Six boiled eggs for breakfast was about right for me, and Andy was fine with three. We hit the trail.

All conditions were good, and Andy is a strong hiker. We made it to Dalton around noon. We ate lunch at McDonald's, and Andy drove me around to re-supply before dropping me off at Tom Levardi's house.

The Badger and Andy

Tom has for decades helped hikers out with a place to stay as well as other valuable favors. There were four of us tonight, the two remaining JerseyBoys and DOS. We got the royal treatment. Tom did our laundry, made a big pasta supper, let us use his shower, put on a movie, and gave us each a bed to sleep in all the while refusing compensation. He'd also driven the other three out of town this morning to slack pack back in. He accepted nothing in return save our company on his front porch where we passed the rest of the evening. Tomorrow I head out for Bennington VT.

—

I was up early, and walking the in-town part of the trail when some important trail business came up. Once again, some of my assets had unexpectedly become liquid, so I hightailed it back to Tom's house. Everyone else was still asleep, so I was able to get everything properly channeled, and was again on my way.

I felt lightheaded, tired, had a splitting headache, and a powerful sense of déjà vu. Even after taking an Aleve, the headache hovered in the background. It was only 75, but I was sweating. I was depressed, but things improved incrementally. By noon, I was feeling so so, and after stopping at an ice cream shop for a root beer float in Cheshire MA, I felt positively normal.

I'm in a big shelter with individual bunks, and a loft. The guys are in the bunks. The women are in the loft. It's on the shoulder of Mount Greylock, the highest peak in Massachusetts. Tomorrow I make my assault on the summit and hope to score a soft drink at the lodge there.

My knee continues to sport a giant knob that is neither painful nor inflamed. I've seen other hikers with similar conditions, and they got better by themselves so it's watch, and wait.

—

Wheeeee!!! Another state just flew by. I'm in Vermont now. I was without malaise or other symptoms and the weather was optimal today. It was 55 when I started hiking, and it never got out of the sixties up on the ridges. There was a good breeze and ranks of cumulus clouds marched up the sky all day giving me shade at least half the time.

I decided to get up when I woke up rather than get up at five sharp so I slept until 5:10. I ate and was off to the summit of Greylock. I got there sometime after eight, and ordered pancakes at Bascom Lodge. I shared a table with a woman from Dallas and her daughter because it was close to an electrical outlet. They were fascinated buy the through-hiking phenomenon and had a ton of questions that I answered all through the meal. Then I took a quick tour of the Massachusetts memorial to its Great War dead before moving on.

I was eating lunch in a breezy clearing with a valley view, sitting on a rock like a gargoyle when a fast moving hiker walked up and asked where the trail continued. I pointed to the place *I* thought it was and he zoomed off only to return 30 seconds later (false trail). He flashed me a Father Christmas look that said, "There'll be a little something extra in your shoe tomorrow morning", but I watched as he left; hah! A Southbounder. I'll never see him again. We're just now seeing the vanguard of the Southbound through-hikers. Weather dictates a May start date for them.

I stopped in North Adams for a liter of Pepsi, which gave me enough energy to get up here to Seth Warner Shelter. I never faltered. Could be low temperatures are all I need.

—

It was in the forties when I woke up this morning, a sign of another good hiking day. It was. I played leapfrog with a father daughter pair out to do the Long Trail. They were faster than I was (naturally) but they stopped a lot, and took a wrong turn once. I took the same turn but sensed bogusness in about 50 yards, and turned back.

They were on the same trail but were so far down it I didn't even hear them. The last time I saw them they'd stopped at Congdon Shelter at 2:30 because they didn't think they'd make it to the next shelter before dark. I assured them that they could do the six miles in three hours, but they seemed dubious. I made it to Vermont Highway 9 a little after four but I had to walk a mile down the road before I got cell service, and called the motel for pickup.

The hotel is a little seedy. The innkeeper's unsmiling wife, looking every bit the harridan, washed my half dozen articles of clothing for four bucks and left them in a plastic bag at the desk. The socks were still wet. Some of the guests have looked at me like they're sizing me up. Bennington however, is quite pleasant. It has a dense little downtown with lots of shops, and restaurants. The big box stores are on the outskirts, out of reach for someone without a car or a lot of time. Fortunately, I don't have any need for them at this stop.

—

When I got up this morning, I checked out what the Mayo Clinic had to say about water on the knee. They covered just about every combination of symptoms but mine (no pain, no inflammation). Of course, there is some ambiguity. Depending on what symptom I've misinterpreted, it could be I have anything from bone rot to terminal flatulence. Still watching, and waiting. I moved the brace with no patella hole to the bad knee so it doesn't look like I have a doorknob sticking out of my knee.

The motel shuttle dropped me off at the trailhead at 7 AM. It was 55 degrees, perfect for the 1500-foot climb out. A grocery bag full of CrackerJack, bags of nuts and a couple of apples was hanging from the map kiosk. I took an apple, which I ate when I reached the first cusp of the ridge. It was delicious.

I encountered the father daughter pair in a tent near the kiosk. They said they had been too tired to climb to the ridge last night. That was the last time I saw them today.

Later on I encountered Magpie whom I hadn't seen since Georgia and I'd never seen her quite so thin. I've seen so many long absent hikers lately. It has me wondering if the woods might once again ring out with the voice of the effervescent Donu[1].

There were many ups and downs, long ups and downs but with temperatures maxing out around 72, it was bearable. I reached Kid Gore Shelter around 6 PM. The shelter is old, and I spotted a couple of mice browsing around the fire ring during dinner. It does have one of the more spectacular views. It looks out over a valley, and a reservoir. It faces due East, so I should see the sunrise this AM.

—

Clouds obscured our view of the sunrise. It was a comfortable 65 degrees, which I feared, might be a portent of a hot day, but it never got out of the seventies above 2000 feet.

My objectives were to climb Stratton Mountain, stay well hydrated, and get as close to Manchester, VT as possible to maximize my re-supply time tomorrow. Stratton Mountain is where in 1925, Benton MacKaye, believing the automobile to be a passing fad, swept his right hand in a wide arc and said, "Let us build a footpath from Maine to Georgia." So it was written, and so it came to be.

---

[1] Donu's mother later wrote to tell me that Donu had left the trail with an injury.

I'm over the mountain now, and eleven miles from the road to Manchester. That will give me most of the afternoon in town before heading to the hostel to shower and do laundry.

This shelter is huge. It sleeps 25. It also costs 5 bucks to stay here. For that money, you get ... to stay here. There's a small Boy Scout troop in for the night. Thankfully they're well behaved.

—

I was the only one up at five, an unusual occurrence of late. I ate and packed alone seeing no one until I was exiting the privy and encountered the only other through-hiker who'd stayed in the shelter last night.

"Could you believe the noise last night?" he said in disgust. I could only smile in reply. I hadn't found the scouts objectionable and this guy had spent the night perfecting his imitation of a sty full of snorting boars.

—

It was a hot day, but I was off the trail and into Manchester Center by one PM thanks to a man in a restored '88 VW van who was going in the opposite direction but gave me a ride anyway! I resupplied and bought food for dinner after which Jeff Taussig, the owner of the Green Mountain House Hostel, picked me up and delivered me here. It's a nice place, spotless with a hiker kitchen sporting all the modern conveniences. Twenty dollars gets you free use of the laundry, kitchen, a pint of Ben and Jerry's, free soft drinks, and the list goes on. I ate my potato salad and a chicken and did my chores.

The younger hikers are watching Goonies on the big screen TV. They're not hitting the trail until

154

9:30. My roommate and I plan to be hiking by 7:00. She's a first year med student trail name of Corbie hiking the Long Trail. She asked how I came to be called Badger. I told her it was my sunny disposition. It's 10:30 PM now. I'm going to die tomorrow if I don't hit the sack.

—

Twenty minutes before it was time to leave, I took my Pepsi out of the refrigerator and stuck it in the freezer. When I heard the car start, I took it out, wrapped it in a foam pad, and buried it in my pack along with a foot long Italian sub. My plan was to have a town lunch on top of a mountain.

My timing was perfect. I made it to Styles Peak at 11:59, but the open spot with a view was also some kind of fly airway. Mostly it was just irritating buzzing, but every once in a while a deer fly would start nipping at me. They have a terrible bite. I was driven into the woods.

Back on the trail, I was plagued by deer flies buzzing my head. I was going to don my hat and bug net but only got as far as the hat. The flies are confused by the brim. They couldn't or wouldn't come under it.

There are many people at Lost Pond Shelter, but I'm the only one staying in the shelter so I can get out early. The biggest group, though tenting, is cooking, and eating at the shelter. This is without precedent in good weather. They did ask if they were keeping me up, and moved out when I said I was going to bed.

Flash: the water is receding from my knee!

Kudos to sister for catching mileage error, brother for keeping me up to date on important, and/or amusing news, and wife for coming up with a fantastic instant spaghetti mix.

—

Just another walk in the woods today. Vermont has been called Vermud. Not much mud right now, but the other appellations, Veroots, and Verocks were appropriate for most of the day.

It wasn't until I started climbing Bear Mountain — did you ever wonder how many bear mountains there are? — that I finally got some good trail. It's a popular day hike so they must have had to reduce danger and inconvenience to socially acceptable levels. The trail was virtually rootless, and rockless with lots of switchbacks. I was over the mountain and down to Minerva Hinchey Shelter in a flash despite the fact that it started raining when I was halfway up. It's supposed to be hot tomorrow so I'm staying in the shelter again for the earliest possible start. The spring here is cold and tasty. I'm going to tank up before I leave.

Stats is here. He left for the next shelter about an hour ago but he returned. He turned down the wrong trail after he left and took about 20 minutes to figure it out.

—

It's been an eventful day. I crossed the 500 miles to go mark, and ran into The Lorax whom I'd last seen getting off the Budget Inn free shuttle in Franklin, NC. He got shin splints in PA, and had to get off the trail for 5 weeks. He's a fast hiker, and I've heard he's handy to have around if your bear bag gets stuck 30 feet up in a tree.

It was easy to see how Stats made the wrong turn. There's a big AT North sign with an arrow pointing down a dirt road. About ten feet down the road, there's a small, unsigned path going off into the woods. If you look down the path, there's a white blaze. It's easy to miss. Anyway, I think Stats was lucky. The trail this morning was treacherous. Last night in the rain, it could have been deadly.

It rained hard twice during the night. I hope it recharged the springs. It certainly bolstered the mosquitoes' morale. They showed up for work bright, and early this morning.

I reached a detour around a trail washout caused by hurricane Irene last year. I'd first heard of it at the Green Mountain Hostel in Manchester Center. It was dismissed by most everyone as unnecessary, but most everyone was in his or her teens or twenties, the same age group that thought the rock climb of death was fun. I pondered my choice over lunch under a crab apple tree. Was I to be a man, and guts the original trail, or a mouse, and take the detour? Well, the cheese in my lunch wrap was absolutely delicious, but I based my decision on the sound reasoning that if trail clubs deem rocky vertical drops safe, then the only way they'd declare a trail unsafe would be when the mangled corpses were turning up faster than they could hide them.

The washed out trail must really be bad, so I took the detour. It turned out to be a good decision. No one was taking the detour, and there was some most excellent trail magic there; a cooler full of soft drinks, and two chairs (with cup holders) to enjoy them in, which I did. My find was made all the better by the fact that I'd encountered two caches earlier in the day that were picked clean. I left a note in the next shelter log recommending the detour to South Bounders.

It took the rest of the day to climb up to Copper Lodge Shelter, which is just shy of 4000 feet. Tomorrow, it's down hill all the way to Rutland, and re-supply.

—

It took forever to get to the highway this morning, but the scenery was nice. I especially liked descending through a grove of paper birch with all those white columns. When I reached the highway it was wicked hot out there on the pavement. I started hitching, and got nowhere until the bus to town showed up. It was two bucks for a ride to the city center; a block away from the Hiker Hostel.

There are towns that try, towns that don't. Towns that fail and towns that succeed. Of all the towns I've passed through on this trek, Rutland surpasses the rest in trying, and succeeding at building a walkable community. Everything in this city of 63,000 can be found downtown including the Wal-Mart.

My plan was to re-supply, take a shower, and a haircut, and bolt, but I was so taken by the place I postponed my departure until tomorrow morning. I got cleaned up, took a haircut from a third generation barber in the original 1935 shop still sporting the original Vermont marble appointments and resupplied in a fraction of the time it normally takes in a big town. Now I have the rest of the day to myself. Maybe I'll buy a house.

Or not. There's a Ford Model-T club show going on. I'll take that in and perhaps a movie, have a leisurely supper, and maybe stop by a tavern for a couple of beers before I turn in. The first bus doesn't leave for the trail until 7:15 AM. I'm staying at The Hiker Hostel in downtown Rutland. It's over the Yellow Delli. Both are owned and operated by a religious group that has been very friendly and helpful. It's low key. One waiter did ask some questions before I even ordered like, "Are you getting everything you need." It felt like he wanted to start a conversation, and he seemed disappointed when I didn't rise to the bait, but that was the end of it.

—

Breakfast was free to hikers at the hostel. I just had an egg sandwich since my weight is now what it was when I started my hike. Then I walked around to the other side of the block to the Marble Valley Transit Authority bus depot where I caught a bus back to the trail.

The big milestone today was reaching Maine Junction where the AT turns East toward New Hampshire, and the Long Trail continues North to Canada. The bad news is that the AT is now running perpendicular to the ridgelines making for a lot of ups and downs. They're not very high, but it adds up in a day. I need to average 15 miles a day to guarantee I can reach the Hanover Post Office before it closes Saturday.

I'd hoped to do better, and get to a shelter so I could make an early start tomorrow but I barely made 15 miles hiking from 7:45 AM to 8:15 PM with only 45 minutes off for lunch and very few breaks. Other hikers complained about making low miles too. It's going to be a tough couple of days getting to Hanover. On the up side, I'm back in my comfy hammock in a birch grove with a cool breeze blowing from Lakota Lake Lookout, and all the bugs are on the outside.

It was tough day crossing ridge after ridge. Some were has high as sixty stories, most were much less but it made for slow going. Some good has come of the Irene damage. The trail was rerouted much closer to a country store, making it well worth a 190 step walk for sodas and ice cream. I met a south bounder there who said to expect 25 percent lower mileage in Maine.

This day also had its ironic moment. All the way through Vermont, we've taken boardwalks through dried up bogs. Today I encountered my first wet bog, and there was no boardwalk. So, tomorrow should be just another long day like this one, except it will put me in New Hampshire.

... and another one bites the dust.

- Queen

I walked into New Hampshire and Hanover this afternoon with plenty of time to pick up my re-supply package from the Post Office. Only two states left! WooHoo!!!

The further I got from the Green Mountains, the smaller the ridges became. I think there was only one Empire State Building sized climb in the lot. Everything went swimmingly until I started looking for a place to stay. Nothing! There are no hostels in town, just two hotels that charge Manhattan five star rates. There are a couple of hotels in nearby towns, but I was too late. They're full up. I ran into MamawB at the post office. She's staying on her ninety year old Aunt's living room floor with Rainbow, and SkunkApe.

There are a number of hiker friendly stores in town where a hiker can get anything from a free snickers bar to a free slice of pizza. I took the free slice, and a few more. As I was leaving the pizza parlor, a mechanical engineering professor from Illinois chatted me up and ended up giving me a ride to the food co-op for re-supply, which was good because they were closing in fifteen minutes. A nice stock clerk walked me to everything I needed. It was the fastest re-supply I ever did.

Then, since I didn't have anyplace to stay, and it was getting dark, I hit the trail which goes into the woods right behind the Dartmouth soccer field. Judging by the number of headlamps dotting the area just inside the woods, a lot of hikers had the same problem and solution I did.

I had a little accident while I was setting up camp. I tripped on a branch, and managed to stab my right hand on a pine branch. It wouldn't stop bleeding until I applied pressure to the wound, and now it is quite painful, but only when I move it or hold it still. The water on my knee is completely gone I'm happy to say. Maybe this new wound is just a replacement.

—

I woke up several times due to the pain in my hand. There didn't seem to be anything I could do to reduce it. Fortunately, by morning, it had gotten to where I could perform fine motor operations without discomfort. It was impossible, however, to use a hiking pole. I stowed the right hiking pole on my pack, and hiked with my hand in a makeshift sling. Going was slow with one less balance point and one less thruster. I went back into town where the nice woman at the co-op garage let me use the bathroom to clean up. Then I struck out for Moose Mountain Shelter. The hand swelled up during the day, peaking around 4:30. It was two hours after that before I could make a fist again. It's just lucky I thrive on adversity, or this could be a real downer. I'll just have to hope I can use a pole again before I hit the White Mountains. I don't think I can make it through them on one pole.

Speaking of downers, it's being reported in the logs that one of the hikers is a thief. He's taken iPods and similar things. He's described as older with curly hair. Let the record show that I have straight hair. In the reunion department, AZCruiser, whom I hadn't seen since Lynchburg Virginia showed up at the shelter and shared a brownie and some dried cherries with me.

—

Swelling returned to my hand during the night, but only on the quadrant where the wound (or stigma) lies. When I changed the dressing, pink tinged brown fluid oozed out. That's good, right?

This was a day of long, steep climbs. First, I climbed a 130-story ridge. It took a little more than an hour. Then I stopped off at Bill Ackerly's house. Bill is known to give hikers water and free ice cream. He wasn't home, but there was a cooler on the porch with 50-cent sodas. I purchased, and guzzled the last one.

Two German boys who'd stayed at the last shelter showed up to get water. They spoke excellent English and from what I could tell, pretty good German. They were headed for this shelter too. I told them the water up here was listed as unreliable which has always meant nonexistent in my experience. I advised them to drink as much water as they could at Ackerly's, and top off their bottles before leaving. They only refilled their bottles, and left.

I took my own advice. When I came to a stream a couple of miles later I made myself some Gatorade and refilled my bottles again. Then I made the steep 210 story climb to the Fire Warden's Cabin cum shelter on Smart Mountain. I met one of the German boys who told me they'd drunk all their water on the way up and surprise, the water source here was dry. I advised him to hike to the stream four miles up the trail and camp there. It's down hill, and they could easily make it there in less than two hours. He accepted this advice but returned in a few minutes saying his friend was too beat to hike. I figured I could give them a pint, which would have me leaving here with no water in the morning. About then, a young couple who'd come up with something like six liters gave the boys enough water for supper, and breakfast.

I actually made good miles today considering. I'm getting adept at hiking with one pole, and can get along as long as the rocks don't get too bad. As with the knee, it's watch, and wait. There's no inflammation except at the immediate site of the wound, just half a hand that looks a tad cherubic.

—

Today consisted of two long climbs. The first was up Mount Cube where I had a scenic breezy lunch with PeppaBoy, a good-natured North bounder on his second through-hike. We agreed that all the ornery hikers seemed to have gotten off the trail early. The second big climb was to Ore Hill Camp where a shelter burned to the ground last year.

The swelling is back to whole hand status. The wound looked so ugly when I took off the bandage that I decided to leave it uncovered to dry out, but it didn't. It just leaked fluids ranging from clear to yellow to brown all afternoon. I've put a pressure bandage on it for the night to see if that will do something. If not, I'll check about seeing a doctor at the hostel tomorrow. Today's kudos go to the Dartmouth Outdoor Club's trail blaze painter for his whimsy, and for returning the bulk of his paint budget to the general fund.

—

It rained crazy hard last night. Either my tarp had some small leaks or the condensation was heavy. It wasn't much, but I stuffed my sleeping bag in a plastic sack just to err on the side of caution. It was warm enough that I didn't need it. One hiker's tent flooded. Good to know before you get to the Whites.

It was a short hike and one quick rain shower on the way down to Glencliff Hiker's Welcome Hostel. I'm in a big co-ed bunkroom. It's not a bad place, but not at all fancy, just adequate I'd say. No freebees except for movies. Braveheart was showing in the common area, which also happened to boast a large collection of Hostess bakery products.

I was enjoying that combination when it came to the part where King Edward, incensed by a young man's outspokenness, tosses him out the tower window. This precipitated a burst of laughter from some college age hikers.

"What?" I said, "That this is a comedy? That was funny?"

164

"Um, sure.'" a young woman replied.

It was one of the few times that the chasm of age yawned broadly on this hike.

The swelling is way down in the hand, and the oozing is pretty much gone too. It's still too painful to use a pole, but on the mend, I think. Tomorrow, I tackle the first of the White's above the tree line, Mount Mousilauke; depending on to whom you talk; it rhymes with HouseLake, LooseMilwaukee or a mixture of the two.

—

When I awoke this morning, it was cold so I hopped out of bed, ate my breakfast bagel, and drank the quart of chocolate milk I'd brought back from the deli, and hit the trail.

The night before the shuttle driver pointed the grim gray outline of Mt. Mousilauke towering 3800 feet above us. I was glad to have the low temperatures. Heat exhaustion would not be a problem this day. At the base of the mountain, I passed the twin tents of ManCub and KitFox. They caught up with me an hour or so later.

I summited at noon. It was cold, windy, and misty. There were a couple of stone walls hikers could use to block the wind. I ate lunch behind one of them. As I did, the mist cleared, and I was treated to some spectacular views. After lunch I headed down what had to be one of the steepest, most dangerous trail I'd ever come across (it's reported to be the most dangerous section of the AT). I didn't have any choice about using two poles. It was painful, and the wound on my hand was soon oozing multicolored fluid again. I encountered a steel bar railing that had come out of it's anchorage at one end. That must have given someone a start. It took forever to get down. There was a trail log box at the bottom. I left a few choice words for the trail club. I'd hiked for ten hours, and come 10.6 miles out of a goal of 15. I need to pick it up if I'm to meet the wife at Crawford Gap on Saturday.

—

It rained today, and the trail was slippery. Once I slipped, and sat down hard. Now I have a sore rump. In another fall I slapped my hand down hard, my *right* hand!!! There were huge slippery rocks to scale all day. It was exhausting. I decided to stop early at Eliza Brook Shelter to give myself the whole day to climb over Kinsman Mountain tomorrow.

The original plan was to go to Crawford Gap, and meet my wife there, but my miles have been so low, at least partly due to my hand, that I won't be able to make it in time so I'm heading for Lincoln. With any luck, I'll be there tomorrow. I'll wait for my wife there and try to get the hand looked at.

My luck isn't looking all that good. I didn't put the complete description of the thief in my journal for obvious reasons. It was definite including a trail name, and the guy who fits it to a T just showed up here.

—

So there we were with a suspected thief in our midst. He certainly was an oddball. Heavy military surplus ALICE pack, canned food, and other outliers; not unheard of or incriminating, but certainly out of the ordinary. His patter, an admixture of treacle and bravado, left me uninterested in getting to know him better.

MrBurns was the first to break with a "Gee, the skeeters was unusual fierce last night. I think I'd better sleep in my tent", and with that, he packed up his gear, and set his tent up a few hundred feet from the shelter. I came in second with "You know, it took me so long to climb over Mousilauke the other day that I think I'd better get a head start on Kinsman", and I did, climbing for an hour to a campsite on the mountain. I ran into the lone holdout, Grok, the next day near the top of Kinsman. He said he didn't feel like packing up, and slept with one eye open.

As I settled in, my hand became increasingly painful. The wound was hard and red, looking like a festering boil. I thought it needed lancing but wasn't up to the task, so I put a waterproof bandage on it knowing it would have the same effect. Two hours later, I made a fist, and pus came gushing out around the bandage. While disgusting, the upshot was transformative. The pain was nearly gone, and in the morning, I could use a hiking pole. The wound is still sore and oozing pus, and needs medical attention as has been advised by several thoughtful observers, but right now, I feel like I'm back to full capability, such as it is.

I came out of the woods in the morning to find MrBurns preparing the paperwork for an important off-trail business transaction. He caught up with me later, and said the "thief" opted to spend another day at the shelter. Maybe he thought he'd have better luck with the next crowd.

—

I met MamawB, PrincessDoah, and Rainbow after lunch and hiked down the mountain to Lonesome Pond Hut, the first of the Appalachian Mountain Club Huts on the AT Northbound. MamawB and Rainbow hung back there. PrincessDoah and I hiked down the mountain to Franconia Notch and caught a shuttle into Lincoln. She dropped me off at a hotel, and went on to a hostel. Tomorrow my good wife will join me, and take me to the emergency room and after that, we'll enjoy a couple of days of R&R.

—

With my wound loaded up with a local anesthetic that definitely wasn't 100% effective, the ER doctor dug and probed for about half an hour until he found a plug of wood nestled up against the other side of my hand. We were all a little shocked at the size of it. It shed pieces as we examined it, and the doctor was virtually certain other bits had been left behind.

I was admitted and wheeled off to the operating room. The anesthesiologist did not use general anesthesia per my request. I prefer to be awake so as to make note of any exclamations of "Ooops!", but he proceeded to fill me with so many drugs that I don't remember a damned thing until I materialized in a bedroom with a dead arm and a hand with bandages so thick it looked like a batch of cotton candy. The surgeon told me he opened the wound up wide, and cleaned out all the junk. Then he packed the now gaping hole with gauze and put me on IV antibiotics. They were going to keep me another day, but just sitting there seemed pointless so we agreed I'd show up at his office tomorrow for an assessment and to work out a forward plan.

We did dinner and a movie before retiring to this hostel, which is also an experiment in "sustainable" non-mechanized farming. The people are very committed and work hard at it, but they seem to have a romantic notion of how it's all supposed to work. I'm not convinced that the very idea is sustainable. Both my wife and I had one or more parents who grew up in this sustainable 19th century model, and found it so harsh that they bailed for the city the first chance they got.

But I won't try to spoil the surprise for these guys. I'm just hoping that the orthopedist can figure something out, a cast maybe, to get my hand stabilized so I can hike with it soon.

—

I saw the doctor today. He removed the bandage and the packing (more pleasant for him than for me). Then he repacked the wound, which was something I wasn't expecting. He wants the healing to take place from the inside to the outside to prevent the abscess from reforming. I left with instructions to repeat the remove/repack process until healing is complete, a process that could take one to two weeks or whatever. I think he meant it will take as long as it takes.

I can still finish my hike if healing takes two weeks. After that we get into a gray area. Anyway, I'm home, and following doctor's instructions. Things haven't changed much around the house. The wind-up clocks aren't running, and the dog, which I'd banned from the bedroom for various and sundry offenses including, but not limited to snoring, farting, loud licking and dream vocalizations has wheedled her way back in. I started to throw her out, but she did such a masterful job of groveling that I'm letting it go for the time being. Other than that, the place is as I left it.

My greatest difficulty now is diet. I'm used to constant food intake whenever I'm off the trail. It's straining my self-discipline to leave food alone except at mealtimes, but it's either that, or carry, and extra five or ten pounds back to New Hampshire.

August, 1816 Miles

Preparation for my return to the trail continues to lurch along pretty much the way the entire endeavor has. The wound in my hand still leaves pus on the packing when I check it, but it looks a little better for what that's worth. If I haven't mentioned it, I do not have a medical degree. Joint pain, a side effect of the antibiotic has manifested itself. Hey, why not?

I'm packing some winter gear; long underwear, my high top boots, and convertible pants. Lastly, I contacted Leki to get a replacement for a bent section of one of my poles. I think it bent while I was using one pole, and put my full weight on it. If I'd called Leki when I first left the trail, I'd have the part by now, but their website didn't have a phone number, and the email I sent them went unanswered. It was only when I checked my AT Guide for a contact that I found a customer service number. The Guide has been an excellent resource.

The drive from Virginia to Lincoln via the byways of the Eastern megapolis takes ten hours. The walk on the AT takes about a month and a half give or take. Driving wins for high stress levels.

Anyway, we're here, and I'm packed, and ready for the 27-mile walk to Crawford Gap. Breakfast is at five AM. I hope to be walking by six, or not too much after. All I need now is some good luck.

Jan dropped me off at about 7 AM. My goal for the day was a shelter 15 miles away, and my backup plan was Garfield Shelter at 10 miles, which is where I am. It took me until 11 PM to get here. I think 16 hours to go 10 miles is a personal worst except for maybe when I sat in a lawn chair all day once. There were virtually no flat spots, just steep ups and downs. I made fairly good time until the last 100 feet or so of Mount LaFayette. It began to rain, and it rained on and off until well after I arrived here.

The rain was horizontal going over the summit as it was going over the myriad minor summits after LaFayette. My glasses fogged over frequently, and the steep descents were treacherous. I slipped frequently, and it was impossible to keep that damned right hand from reflexively flying out to break my fall. It took about an hour to come down the last 300 feet in altitude over a quarter mile. Visibility was much too poor to venture into the woods to look for a campsite, and I was afraid I might miss the turn-off, and have to spend the night sitting under a tree wrapped in my tarp. This disaster had debacle written all over it.

When I got here, it was raining harder than I've ever experienced in my lifetime. I couldn't read the Garfield Shelter sign until I was within six inches of it. The side trail to the shelter was under four inches of water. I was relieved that there was plenty of room, and that the peg wall for gear storage was well away from the sleeping area. That's a rarity.

One of the guys was a snorer, but it didn't bother me too much. I was way too tired. There was water in my pack, but I have everything in waterproof sacks so I had dry clothes to change into for sleeping. It won't be easy to put the wet ones back on in the morning.

—

It took all morning to cover the 2.5 miles to Galehead Hut. The huts differ from shelters in that they're manned, have bunks, and serve meals.

My mileage was so low that I wouldn't have enough food to make it to Crawford Gap; so again, I needed to get out to re-supply. The crew chief showed me the service trail on his map. It was relatively benign compared to what I'd been struggling with, but I still couldn't make any speed. Even after I made it to flat terrain along the Gale River, it was all I could do to throw my legs forward. My knees were killing me. It took all afternoon to cover the 4 miles to the trailhead where Jan was waiting to pick me up.

When I was a pilot, I had to be alert for something we called "GetHomeItis", a condition wherein pilots, anxious to reach their destination, downplay the importance of deteriorating weather, engine parts lying on the tarmac, and similar contraindications to safe flight, and take to the air, occasionally with fatal results.

I'm ashamed to say that I fell victim a few times before I got Religion. It made for a couple of interesting flights. I seem to have contracted something similar called "Katahdinitis". I've been downplaying injuries and mounting infirmities to justify continuing to the end of the AT and the results have been progressively less productive.

I mulled this over, and decided it's time to give it a rest. I am this day declaring 1800 miles, and change a great victory for me, my race, and all the

English-speaking peoples. As such, I am folding my tent, and going home to heal. I'll finish this hike next year.

July, the Next Year, 1829 Miles

I'm back on the trail after nearly a year off, and I feel great. My morale is high, and I'm physically whole again. My friend Heinrich has joined me for the first two weeks. The plan was to post at my journal Joe Dodge Lodge but there was an incompatibility between the lodge system and my IPhone 5 so I had to wait for Gorham, NH.

I had an uneventful flight save for the extra intimate pat down from the DHS inspectors. They were probably concerned that I had no luggage which may have had them thinking I was planning to only go half way. They also swabbed my knee braces with an explosive detecting wand. It's reassuring to know they're not going to explode if I work them too hard.

SitABit, whom I'd encountered last year, met me at the airport. He'd met Heinrich earlier, and fed him lunch. Then he drove us to the trail an hour and a half away. I'm hard pressed to think of someone who's been as generous with his time as SitABit. Due to the hour of our arrival at the trailhead, the plan was to hike into the woods a mile or so, and camp for the night, but we made good time, and soon arrived at Galehead Hut — where last year I turned tail, and scurried South as fast as my skinny little bandy legs would carry me — in time to watch the sunset. All my conditioning combined with being ten pounds lighter than last year, and getting about four pounds out of my pack paid off. I was wafting through the woods like a skeeter in a summer zephyr.

The hut is fully booked but I asked the hut supervisor if we could crash on the dining room floor. He was cool with that, we just have to leave our packs outside until lights out at 9:30, and then stake out a spot between the tables. Tomorrow, an easy walk to Zealand Hut where we have reservations for bunks, dinner, and breakfast.

—

A chorus of snorers kept me awake a good part of the night. It was only today that I learned that the huts started giving out free earplugs this year. I'm armed with a pair tonight. It was a relatively quick but tiring walk to Zealand from Galehead. We arrived just after lunchtime. We both took a solid nap before spending a rare afternoon of leisure.

Dinner was served family style. It was generous and delicious. The place was full, and the crowd was social. I sat next to three gregarious women I'll dub The Three Amigos who were hut hiking and enjoyed an hour of cheerful chatter. Their mode of hiking, being out for a few days, packing several box 'o wines, hiking short distances, and staying in huts that feed them breakfast and dinner is much more civilized than the way I hike, but I think I could get used to it.

It was announced that an AT through-hiker would give an after dinner lecture about the AT experience. I think I'll give it a miss and read as much as I can of Bryson's "At Home" before I have to leave it in the hut library.

—

We got an early start by skipping the breakfast that came with our stay at Zealand. This was to be our longest day before we meet DreamTime's partner, Andy on the 17th. We had great hiking from Zealand to Crawford notch. It was all abandoned logging roads and an old railroad bed.

We made 8 miles by lunchtime and took the rest of the day to go the remaining six. We started climbing out of Crawford Notch right after lunch. It was a vertical half mile with many rock scrambles and climbs of doom. Once we were on top, the trail that had looked benign on the profile was actually an unending series of steep ups and downs. It was slow going.

Heinrich on climb of doom

The high point of the afternoon was getting cell service for the first time since we started when we were about two miles from the hut. I texted Jan and Andy. It would have been nice to post my journal for the first time since we started but it was getting late, and we still had a ways to go. We also caught glimpses of Mount Washington, which we will go over tomorrow. We're at a campsite near Mizpah Hut now. Huts cost one hundred twenty dollars a night, so we only planned a stay at Zealand.

—

It was a long day. We scored free pancakes at Lakes of the Clouds Hut, and summited Mt. Washington at noon, ate lunch at the restaurant there and got rid of our trash. The mountains were shrouded in mist so we didn't see much.

The sun came out in the afternoon treating us to the best alpine views so far. Unfortunately, the trail was crap. It was one rock scramble after another which made for slow going. We made Madison Hut at about six thirty, the hut master was an aspiring harridan who only let young through-hikers crash in the dining room. We had to hike another half mile down a steep rocky ravine to this tent site only to find it was full.

Fortunately, the last site had been taken by a young couple through-hiking South bound with their dog. They made room for Heinrich's tent, and I hung from some nearby trees. Heinrich crashed without eating anything. I made my dinner, and chatted with our hosts, Funk, and BoJangles. They're from Virginia, graduates of Virginia Tech and very thoughtful.

I'm pretty tired myself. It was all I could do to brush my teeth, and get my bear bag up. I left the tarp off my hammock for the first time ever. Time to do a little star gazing and sleeping.

—

This day started well enough. Funk had expressed doubt about dining atop Washington because they had to husband their resources. She was sleeping when we left, but when she awoke, she would find enough money for a good meal on Washington in her shoe. They should thank SitABit for that because when we offered to reimburse him for his expenses he wouldn't hear of it. He just said, "Pay it forward!"

It was down hill (figuratively speaking) from there. It was the most arduous walk yet. The Osgood Trail (coincides with AT) runs along a long, sharp, rocky ridge. The rocks were big and pointy with huge gaps between them making the traverse both treacherous, and painful. The heat was such that I couldn't drink enough water to stay hydrated. I didn't pee all day.

By the time we got to better trail as we descended toward Pinkham Notch, we were bushed, and Heinrich was lagging behind. I had to stop a couple of times to let him catch up.

We cleaned up, and rested when we got to the Notch. We registered at Joe Dodge Lodge, and ate dinner family style with the other guests. The conversation went mostly to hiking issues with forays into defense contracting and plant genetics; the latter with a German couple Heinrich buttonholed. We had a forest ranger at our table who explained why the trails in the Whites had a dearth of switchback trails. She said that the trails were laid out before erosion control was understood.

We had a great time, but after dinner, Heinrich announced he was worn out and had decided to leave the trail early. I told him I thought it was a sound decision. There's no point in making matters worse. I really enjoyed his company, and was sorry to see him go, but I won't be hiking alone just yet. Andy will be joining me tomorrow, and so will his partner DreamTime. It's going to be Old Home Week.

—

I bade farewell to Heinrich, and he caught a bus to Boston this morning. As I walked back to the Lodge, I heard DreamTime calling my name. She and her husband Andy will be hiking with me as far as Andover, Maine.

Andy, The Badger and DreamTime

They were disappointed that they wouldn't meet Heinrich. DreamTime admonished me for planning 10-mile days with him. In retrospect, she was right. He'd have had a better chance to become acclimated, and even if he still left, the experience would have been better. In my defense, it must be said that I'm an insensitive lout who cannot be expected to know such things.

We got on the trail at about nine. It was the usual sheer rock faces of death and staircases of doom punctuated with the occasional stunning vista on the 200-story climb out. We arrived at Carter Hut an hour before dinnertime. They served a big but not wholly satisfying meal (not enough fat), and I met several interesting people. MidwesternMamma and PaintedLady, who've been section hiking for years invited me to slack pack with them for a few days after DreamTime and Andy leave the trail. Slack packing consists of being dropped off up the trail, and hiking back with only a daypack. It is incredibly easy. When I did it last year in Connecticut, I finished what was normally a day's hike by noon. Things are looking up.

—

It was a hard hike to Imp Camp site, but with almost none of the dangerous obstacles we encountered yesterday. We just powered along, and got here at about four thirty. We had plenty of time to clean up, and get dinner ready. DreamTime and Andy are sharing a platform so I invited them to mine where there would be more room to cook. We ate a leisurely dinner after which we set about battening down our shelters for a storm that's expected sometime during the night. They're expecting 50 mph winds on the mountaintops, but we're in a ravine, protected by trees, and just need to make sure our shelters are prepared for rain. I'm all set *(boy was I wrong about that!)*. Tomorrow it's supposed to be an easy walk to the hostel situated at the trailhead in Gorham, NH.

—

I woke around 11 PM to the Hammock bouncing up and down, something unique in my experience.

Gentle swinging yes, up and down, no. I looked outside, and saw tree trunks swaying at ground level; also unique in my experience. I was quite comfortable in the hammock but I got to thinking that one of those trees could sway over on top of me. I decided there was no need to hang around to watch it happen, so I grabbed my sleeping bag, my mattress and my pillow, and hightailed it for the shelter.

I let Andy and DreamTime know what I was doing as I passed their platform. They said they were staying put. It was pretty crowded in the shelter but a girl on the first level pulled her stuff closer, and I laid down between her and the front wall. About fifteen minutes later Andy and DreamTime showed up having reconsidered their options. The hikers on the second shelf were spaced about a foot apart, and could easily have made room, but they weren't budging. DreamTime had started giving them what for when the girl who made room for me gathered her stuff even closer so DreamTime could shoehorn herself in next to me. Someone at the other end of the shelter did the same for Andy. I woke again at one AM to calm air, and moved back to the hammock. We left camp at about 7:30. It was to be my best hiking day yet despite gouging my forehead on a pine branch and taking a couple of spectacular dives into the dirt (landing on my pack fortunately). My energy seemed boundless. Instead of stopping at rock faces, and laboriously clawing my way up, I'd run at them, and let my inertia carry me up and over. We covered 8 miles, and were out of the woods just after 12:30 PM. I did the last two miles at a blistering 3 mph.

The trail comes out right by the White Mountains Hostel. I registered, showered, put on clean clothes, and was off to town to *finally* post my journal entries for the week, and upload a few photos. High speed internet must be in short supply in Gorham because the entire computer owning population had gathered at the McDonald's and set up their laptops, and in the process, usurped the one outlet near a table. Fortunately, I beat the spillover to the only other restaurant with Wi-Fi, and spent the next two hours nursing a glass of milk while uploading under the glowering eyes of disappointed outlet coveters.

When I'd finished, I took time to wander around town. Gorham is wholly dependent on the tourist trade. One resident told me that when the season ends, the town folds up like a cheap suit. I don't know how cheap suits fold, or if there's any difference between that, and expensive suit folding, but I got the impression it wasn't good. Things really went to hell when the recession hit and recovery has been painfully slow. Nevertheless, the residents are putting the best face they can on it. Most buildings are freshly painted and otherwise well tended. I went to dinner with WornHeel, a shoemaker, DreamTime, and Andy. I was careful to eat too much, and drink too little before returning to the hostel to sort laundry, which the proprietors, Jeri and Greg, had washed for free. They also ran shuttles to town and the Wal-Mart and served a big breakfast all included in the $36 a night rent. Jeri and Greg bought the place four years ago, but now have it up for sale because of the unremitting demands the business places on them. Maybe they'd find it easier if they charged for some of the free services.

—

We were out of the Hostel at 7:30 with heavy packs. We'd just resupplied, and were carrying a head of Romaine, apples, and a red bell pepper. Heinrich originated this idea. We inherited his lettuce on the last leg, and it was still fresh after three days in a pack so we bought more.

It was a high mileage day for this part of the trail. Fatigue set in near the end of the day, and I took a drop and roll fall that DT and Andy found amusing.

As we came abreast of the pond we spotted a moose cow — We'd been watching for moose in the ponds because we'd been encountering scat piles (think a bucket full of Milk Duds) all day — and her calf on the side opposite the trail. That's my first live moose sighting ever! I took a telephoto shot, and a definite moose shape is visible in the distance. Before I forget, we saw a great blue heron ridge soaring when we topped Wildcat.

MidwesternMamma showed up late in the day sans PaintedLady. It seems PL had misgivings about going through Mahoosuc Notch. The Notch is a large, mile-long boulder jumble that I ain't so keen about traversing myself. MM wants to cast her lot with us now. We're good with it, but MM is considerably slower, and hiking at her pace may result in a food shortage. We have a plan we think will work. We hope to reach the notch the day after tomorrow.

—

We crossed into Maine today. It is the last state we have to conquer unless you include my state of mind. It was a day in which again, we averaged about one mile per hour. There was nothing particularly dangerous, just countless times when we would top a mountain, see another higher peak across a wide, deep valley, and know we'd be making yet another steep descent and long steep climb over boulder-strewn trails.

I had it a little easier today. I was using bicycle gloves I'd purchased in Gorham. They have gel pads. One of them covers the incision scar in my right hand, making it a lot less sensitive to pressure. They certainly might have changed the outcome of last year's hike.

MidwesternMamma caught up, and hiked with us for a while. She seemed increasingly distressed about hiking the Mahoosuc Notch. I'm not sure why. She'd be hiking with us. DreamTime hiked it alone last year without incident, and it's not as though a body count is racking up over there. She left us to get water at an off-trail spring. A late arrival here brought word that MM had decided to call it quits. Sad for her and it looks like I won't be slack packing with that group. We should hit the Notch early tomorrow morning.

Into the valley of death ...

I've been asked to convey as much information about work-for-stay at the White Mountain Huts. I can't say much because I didn't benefit. If you're slow, you will notice nineteen year olds shooting past you like flies homing on a fetid pit toilet. They're the ones who arrive in time to get one of two official work-for-stay billets. There's also do-nothing-for-stay, which is crash on the dining room floor and no food. It isn't officially sanctioned. The

185

Galehead Hut Master figured as long as there was space, it might as well be put to good use. The Madison Hut master allowed those she fancied to stay, and sent the rest packing. I suppose I could have invoked my super power of invisibility to young women and crashed anyway, but it's only supposed to be used for the greater good, not anything so vulgar as the advancement of one's self interest. I'm sorry I can't be of more help.

The rain started around 4 AM, and kept up for most of the day. The trails, which were little more than rock jumbles, and steep slabs served as run-off channels. We reached Mahoosuc Notch, billed as the most difficult mile of the trail at 9:15. For once all the hype wasn't hype. You could see where the entire side of the mountain on the right had sheared off, and crumbled into the ravine leaving a jumble of rocks varying from pea to semi-trailer sized rocks. Cold air blasted from chasms filled with last winter's ice, and frigid run off stiffened fingers and numbed feet. The risk of walking with hiking poles was too high. We stowed them and climbed over and under the wet rock on all fours, occasionally needing to doff our packs to push them ahead through low rock tunnels. Had I not known the length of the ravine, I'd have turned back after 100 yards. We emerged at a campsite by a river after a little over two hours. We put up my tarp, and ate lunch under it. We ate as fast as we could because we were soaked through, and needed to keep moving. And move we did. Almost straight up the gushing stream that was the Mahoosuc Arm trail. It was exhausting work made more so because my arms ached from the strains placed on them in the Notch.

Had it been a pleasant day, we'd have continued another 7 miles to Bald Pate, but cold and fatigue dictated we stop at Speck Pond Shelter at 3:30 where we commandeered a group tent platform. Andy and I hung our hammocks over the ends, and Dreamtime's tent is sandwiched in between. Tomorrow we plan to hike to a road a few miles up the trail to meet our transportation to a hostel where we can dry things out, and get a pizza. I'm wasting away on trail food.

—

I waited until the last second this morning to change out of my camp clothes into my freezing wet hiking togs. As soon as we got moving, I warmed up pretty well but wet clothes are wet clothes. We called DreamTime's friend Vern from her hiking club from the top of Old Speck Mountain, and he picked us up where the AT crosses a highway.

Vern is putting us up, and will slack pack us for a few days. We had pizza for lunch then Vern dropped me at a McDonald's so I could post. I was the only person using the Wi-Fi. I got the feeling that they were discouraging over use because the only outlet in the dining room was located at the very top of the wall. I wasn't bothered because I could charge my electrics at Vern's. They picked me up two hours later, and we went out for dinner.

On the way back to Vern's cabin, we took a detour to visit the local wind farm. It's difficult to convey the scale of the windmills. The tower is 300 feet tall, and the blade extends another 137 feet. For all the caterwauling I've heard about the sound, I found it barely noticeable, even standing directly underneath. At Vern's cabin, I occasionally heard a faint swishing on the porch, but nothing when I went inside.

Tomorrow, our first slack pack!

—

As we were descending Bald Pate (spectacular 360 views), there was a big commotion behind me. I turned to see Andy flailing down the rock face. He couldn't make the turn where the trail did so he plowed into the woods at full rip. He managed to snag a sapling, which bent over 90 degrees but didn't break, and came to a stop yelling "I'm Okay!" When he regained more composure he said he'd tripped on something, and there was nothing for it but to try to outrun gravity to keep his feet under him. I thought he did a good job of it.

We put on some good miles slack packing today, but nothing nearly as impressive as we managed in Connecticut last year. The above and other incidents increased the level of fastidiousness when it came to foot placement all of which takes time. It was 5:30 by the time we got out of the woods, and my knees were in a hurt because I'd neglected to bring NSAIDS along. Vern had hiked in to meet us so we had immediate transportation to dinner followed by a visit to an ice cream shoppe in Andover and a round of unsuccessful moose stalking. Tomorrow we do another slack pack.

—

This was our last day of slack packing, and the easiest hiking we've had. There was one steep, high climb but no giant blocks of stone or steep rock faces. We were out of the woods at South Arm Road by 4 o'clock. A couple of South Bounders were waiting for a ride so we took them into town with us.

It was early for dinner so we bought a six-pack of ale and drank it in the gazebo on the Andover village green. Vern didn't know if it was legal but he knew that there are no town police.

Andover is a block long with a couple of convenience stores and restaurants. As with so many trail towns, the economy is depressed. It's not always a completely bad thing. Prime Rib at the little Red Hen cost me $17.

When we were sitting down to dinner, DreamTime recognized Angelo Kaltsos, author of "The Outhouse Chronicles" and several other books and invited him to dine with us. He is a charming man of 83 with a rich life experience. We had a pleasant time culminating with a walk down the block to the ice cream parlor. Then it was back to Vern's to pack and be ready for the trail tomorrow.

—

After breakfast this morning, I said goodbye to DreamTime, Andy, and Vern when they dropped me off at the trailhead. I had a great time with them, and they gave me a good start on my final run to Mount Katahdin. They were all very generous with their time and resources. I can't thank them enough.

The weather was perfect for hiking; sunny, cool, and probably the clearest it's been in weeks. Climbing Old Blue I saw the wind farm near Vern's cabin with stark clarity. The views from atop the Bemis Peaks were also well worth the climb. I had good cell service all day. I sent Andy a couple of emails only to get an automated reply from his office. I'm going to try text but he didn't get the ones I sent him from the Whites.

My goal today was Bemis Lean-to. I got there at about 4:30 which DreamTime and I agree is ideal, but with no one else there I decided to hike a few more miles to this campsite. I'm meeting up with my nephew and his family at Rangely. Getting there a day earlier than planned will let me take a zero day with them.

I'm sharing this site with a South Bounder named Ben. He told me he found a message at a road crossing from DT, Andy & Vern congratulating me on getting that far. I'll look for it in the morning.

—

My bear bag line got hung up in the tree when I went to retrieve my food this morning. It wouldn't come down even with my full weight on it so I decided to climb up and free it after fortifying myself with breakfast. The line is 2 mm Spectra 300 lb. test. Who wouldn't risk their life for that? I told Ben of my plan half hoping that the image of a frail codger climbing a spindly maple would spur him to action but he didn't bite. It was up to me.

Ben came over to watch when I was about ten feet up. I suggested he stand directly under me so he could break my fall and he actually did!

I said, "Just kidding! Get back!"

The tree was down to 2 inches diameter, and starting to sway when the snag was about a yard from my reach. It dampened my enthusiasm for climbing higher so I got Ben to tie a stout stick to the free end of the line, which I then hauled up.

After much beating, poking, cursing, and begging the line came loose. I thanked Ben, and we went our separate ways. I found the note from DreamTime Et. Al. under a cairn at Height of Land.

The trail was in good shape. I made record speed and was on the highway hitching into Rangely by ten to five.

I enjoyed a zero day in Rangely with extended family.

—

My nephew dropped me off at the trailhead at 9:30. It was an absolutely beautiful day, and with only 8 miles planned, I was taking my time. All went well until after lunch when I met DragonFly. He said he was a North bounder. So why was he headed South? Things clicked pretty quickly as I realized *I* was the one headed South. I remembered coming to a split in the trail. One fork headed for a pond, and the other had a white blaze on it. I took the white blaze even though the direction seemed wrong. Just before that, I had, without knowing it, gotten off on an old section of the AT that had been decommissioned. The fork was where it rejoined the new AT.

That little mistake cost me thirty or forty minutes. Since I only planned on eight miles, it wasn't a big deal. I got to Reddington Camp around 5:30 and set up camp by the numbers. It was half a mile round trip for water. I put up the hammock, set my food bag line, and fixed dinner. I was having cous cous. I made some last year, and it was almost too bland to eat so this time I added a packet of turkey gravy; much better! I had cherry pie for desert. The bear bag is hung, it's sixty-two and windy, and I'm off to bed.

It was in the forties when I woke, and I didn't want to change into hiking clothes. It took me two hours to eat, and break camp. Once out, my right foot began to hurt. It felt like one of the bones wanted to push out the side of the shoe. I didn't feel like I was fully awake either.

As I descended from Little Saddleback, I spotted a woman with her back to me. I said hello as faintly as possible so as not to startle her. There was no reaction. I said hello much louder, still nothing so I yelled. Nothing! I whistled the loudest I know how. It's so loud it once silenced a theater packed with raucous college boys watching a Linda Lovelace Movie (I was frustrated. They were drowning out important exposition). Still nothing so I slowly and carefully insinuated myself into her field of view which gave her a start. I said hello again but she just smiled without saying anything, and I moved on.

About one hundred yards further down, I encountered a man painstakingly picking his way up the trail. Again, I said hello, and again there was no answer. He didn't even make eye contact, but that's not altogether unusual out here. I moved to one side to let him pass. As he did, he pushed against me as if I were a tree or a rock. He was startled at first by my movement, then he stared intently, smiled, and made some hand gestures to indicate that vision, and hearing were not his long suits. His attention returned to the trail, and as he hiked on I noticed his attire other than his pack and poles was more that of a roller blader than a hiker. He wore a helmet, wrist, and shin guards. I thought of all the rock faces of death and stairs of doom that lay ahead and was a little frightened for him.

But he does appear to have a partner to scrape him off the rocks, stand him up, and point him in the right direction with a pat on the fanny. Who needs more than that?

There are a dozen or so North bounders at Spaulding Mountain Lean-to tonight; all young; all hiking close to twenty miles a day, and can't wait to finish. Their food bags weigh more than my whole pack, but they all spoke their awe of the blind hiker they met today.

August, 2001 Miles

I was on my way at 7:15 AM. I reached Crocker Cirque Campsite, my goal for the day before noon so I decided to shoot for Stratton, my intended re-supply town. Instead of cooking lunch, to save time I ate 900 calories worth of blueberry Pop Tarts, cherry pie, and Gatorade, and lit out for Stratton.

I was on the backside of North Crocker Mountain with nothing but downhill between me and town when I found a camera lying on the trail. I was able to ascertain what the owner looked like, the number in his party, and his direction from the pictures. I was headed the same way so I took it with me. Sometime later, I came across two hikers fixing a meal. I said, "There wouldn't happen to be three of you would there?" The answer was no. I told them I found a camera that belonged to someone hiking with two other guys. They said they hadn't seen a group like that.

Actually, the owner of the camera was the one with his back to me. The third guy had bailed two days ago. These two geniuses concluded that since there were only two of them now, it couldn't be their camera. I moved on. Half an hour later, the owner discovered his camera was missing so the two of them stepped through their original logic, found it wanting, and set out after me.

Meanwhile I was floating down the trail buoyed by what a good person I was for making such a heroic effort to find the camera's owner. Surely, this would put the seal on my beatification. I fantasized a grateful owner saying, "Anything you want! You name it!", and me demurring, "Shucks, you don't owe me nuthin', but I wouldn't say no to a cheeseburger." About that time, I heard someone shout, "You have my camera!" I turned to see an exhausted owner — he'd been chasing me for an hour — looking like he'd been shot in the gut; breathing his last. I asked him how he managed to get behind me. When he recovered his breath, he recounted the events.

He couldn't stop thanking me. He asked if he could take my picture. I said, "Sure!" The look on my face in the photo was clearly one of a man thinking, "I *am* a nice person!"

I reached the trailhead at 5:30, and begged a ride to town from a man in the parking lot. Stratton is a good trail town. All the services are within a 500-foot radius. The grocery store has tons of hiker food including electrolyte tablets and condiments in individual serving packets. I haven't seen that since Hot Springs, NC. The Stratton Motel offers laundry and trail shuttles at six and nine AM. Doesn't get any better than that!

—

It rained during the night but it stopped for a while to give everyone hope that the front had passed. It started pouring again during breakfast. I had an hour to re-supply, and eat breakfast before the last shuttle left at nine. I did pretty well but, in my haste, I forgot a brick of cheese. That will be a nine hundred calorie deficit on this leg. I did pack half a pound of butter, which should offset the loss. This is important because I'm darned near out of adjustments on my pack again meaning that I'm under weight.

There were seven hikers in the diner this morning but only one on the shuttle; me. The rest decided to wait out the rain. For some reason a lot of hikers have a phobia about sweating in their rain gear. They don't mind sweating until they're dripping wet if they don't have rain gear, but will cancel plans until better weather if it keeps them from sweating in their rain jackets. Since it wasn't windy, I put the jacket hood on my head, and let the rest drape over my pack. It quit raining mid-morning. The rest of the day I hiked with thunder boomers all around me but none overhead except one as I came abreast Horn's Pond Lean-to's so I ducked in for a few minutes to let it pass.

I'd have signed the log but half the shelters don't have one. A female North bounder has been missing for more than a week. Search and Rescue might have a better idea where to look if there'd been logs. Of course many people don't bother to sign in. I don't know if that's the case for the missing hiker. I talked to WornHeel over a beer last night. He said he heard something that sounded like a moan but got no answer when he responded. He didn't investigate further but did report it when he got to town. The woman's husband said it was the first good lead they'd had so he paid for WornHeel's bunk at the Stratton Motel[1].

—

---

[1] The poor woman was still alive, languishing in her tent by a stream about three miles from the trail. She wrote in her journal that she'd become disoriented during a bathroom break, and got lost in very dense woods. She starved to death, and wasn't found until the following year.

Avery Memorial Campsite is in a small notch between the first two Bigelow peaks. I was alone at first but the young couple MilesToGo and Flash showed up as I was starting dinner. They're much faster than I am but they waited out the rain in Stratton. I didn't ask why. I assume it had something to do with sweat.

I was cold last night. It got into the forties, but I think my forty-degree quilt might only be good to about fifty. It started raining as I was leaving camp, which was good because when I reached the Avery Peak of the Bigelows it was cold and windy. I was glad to have the rain pants and jacket on. The views from Avery were terrific, but I didn't linger.

Once I got off the Bigelows, the terrain flattened out, and the trail got soft. It was smooth sailing for the rest of the day. I got to East Flagstaff Lake around four, and considered doing a few more miles but after I saw the place, I didn't want to leave. It would be a good place to zero if I had company. I can see the sun glinting off the lake through the trees from my hang. It's a short walk down to the beach, which has beautiful mountain and water views. I cooked and ate dinner on the beach. It could have been ruined by a deer fly. You can't ignore them. The little shits are relentless. They have a painful bite, and the welt it raises itches intensely for hours. I swatted and assaulted it with the foulest insults I know to no avail, but it finally made the tactical error of flying into my food bag, presumably to check out the odor of summer sausage.

WHAM! Deer fly and Pop Tarts pulverized. No matter. The Pop Tarts still have their calories and the fly is dead. The rest of dinner was idyllic. I thought of MilesToGo and Flash. They skipped this campsite because they're anxious to get to Katahdin. If I owned this plot, Katahdin could wait forever.

—

The trails were easy today. In fact, I've seen handicapped accessible trails that were worse. To put it another way, this was the AT I was born to hike. I could have easily made it to the town of Caratunk for re-supply but the Kenebec River ferry (a canoe) closes at 4 PM, which is about when I'd have gotten there if I didn't encounter bad trail. It wasn't worth the risk.

Instead, I stopped at a sports lodge that was built in 1932. It's been run by Tim for the last 25 years. It's a good-sized place with a central lodge with toilets and showers, and rustic cabins with oil lamps, a table, and beds. Tim does everything himself except when he gets a big party so needless to say, it's getting a bit frayed, but it still retains a great deal of charm.

Hikers staying in the shelter a few tenths back up the trail can pre-pay for breakfast. That's what I was going to do, but when I stopped in to make the reservation I found out that for a few bucks more I could have a cabin, and a hot shower and also save myself the walk back to the shelter and back in the morning. Then Tim gave me a free ice-cold coke and a piece of blueberry muffin cake. That sealed the deal.

My cabin sits just above some rapids, and the sunset will be visible from my porch. Tim fired up the generator so I can charge my electrics. I cooked my dinner on the porch of my cabin before going up to the lodge, and sitting on the porch with Tim. He shared his wine with me, and we watched the dozen or so humming birds at his feeders until it was time to turn in.

—

Tim made a big breakfast. We got 12 pancakes each loaded with fruit, coffee, juice eggs, and sausage. I sat with four gentlemen from Georgia who were completing a sixteen year section hike of the AT this year.

After breakfast, it was off to the Kenebec River where we arrived to be the second set of ferry passengers of the day. The landing wasn't far from Caratunk. I resupplied there in about twenty minutes, and was back on the trail. I didn't even take time to post my journal.

The reason for the rush was that I miscalculated the distance to Monson, and thought I could be there tomorrow if I made it to this lean-to. When I got here I re-calculated, and to my dismay, found that it's 22 miles to Monson. It would take some sweet trails or a real emergency to get that far. No matter. Jan won't get there until Wednesday at the earliest. One or more zeros are planned.

—

As soon as I realized I wouldn't get to Monson today, I should've moved out of the shelter. I set up in there to save the time it takes to break camp in the morning. Inertia is my enemy. I hardly slept all night, and felt tired all day.

I called Jan from the top of Moxie Bald to get her plans then I set about making the miles I needed to make. It wasn't easy. I got turned around again. I caught it quickly, and carefully retraced my steps to a fork with a white blaze on the left branch and a white blaze on the right branch. The left branch looked familiar so this time I took the right. For the rest of the day I was second-guessing myself, wondering if I'd missed another turn and was headed in the wrong direction. Hey Maine Appalachian Trail Club; other clubs obliterate all the blazes on retired sections of the trail, and erect substantial debris barriers at both junctions. I think this might work for you too. I got to Horseshoe Canyon Lean-to at four. Despite being early, I decided to stay if there was anyone else in the shelter, but the place was deserted, so I hiked to this river that I'll need to ford in the morning. By camping here, I can put on my rubber fording shoes when I get up, and get across the river instead of having to change out of my hiking shoes. That takes longer than you'd think.

ZZTopless, who usually sleeps in until ten, and passes me around noon just walked into the last ford with his hiking boots on. He's not bothered by wet boots. I am.

When I got here, the moskwitos immediately formed a thick cloud around me. I squirted on just enough DEET to keep them at bay while I built a smoldering fire. It's amazing how well that clears a site and keeps it clear. I ate dinner in peace and got into my hammock before they returned.

It's about eight miles to Monson. I should get there well ahead of Jan tomorrow.

—

I was freezing when I got up this morning. I scotched my quick fording plans and put on every stitch I own while I did breakfast and packed up. I was fine as soon as I started moving, and I got into Monson around eleven.

Monson is the gateway to the hundred-mile wilderness. There's nothing quite like a frontier town. The hustle, the bustle, the busy outfitters, throngs of frontiersmen moving up and down Main street, the raucous taverns, the crowded boarding houses; all the things that Monson is not. If other trail towns are depressed, Monson has been hammered flat. Jan and I headed for the General Store, listed in the guide as a full re-supply store. Tacked to the front door was a three by five card with three words scrawled thereon. "Out of Business"! Not good news for someone facing 10 days in the boonies with two powdered pop tarts and a quarter bag of Tang in his pack. The only extant businesses aside from a couple of hostels are two restaurants and a gas station that sells limited re-supply items.

Fortunately, at least one of the hostels, Shaw's, is a vibrant, well-run inn. It's packed with hikers, section and through. It's clean. It offers free use of laundry, AYCE breakfast with stay and cans of soda for fifty cents! They picked Jan up at Bangor International, an hour and a half away for seventy bucks, and they offered to drive us to a supermarket in the next town later today!

Shaw's is also for sale. The owners have been at it for eight years, which seems to be at the long end of hostel ownership. Running a hostel holds an undeniable romantic appeal for many of us. When I saw the sign in the yard my first thought was, "Gee, I wonder how much they want for it". Fortunately, a little voice said, "There's a reason why so many hostels are for sale". That reason being that the owners wake up one day realizing that they're killing themselves for peanuts. Well, I hope they find a buyer, preferably one of those rare birds like

Tim of Pierce Pond Sporting Camps who are suited to the life.

It's pouring today. There are half a dozen hikers on the side porch peering skyward hoping for a lull. We won't head out until tomorrow. The forecast is sunny.

—

Rain drove hikers off the trail and filled Monson with so many backpackers that the hostels couldn't hold them all, forcing some to shuttle out of town. There isn't a lot to do here. We tried the barbecue place for lunch. It was pretty good.

After lunch Shaw's shuttled four of us to the supermarket in Greenville for a decent re-supply. Jan had the brilliant idea of asking the deli section if they had mayonnaise packets, and they gave her all we wanted gratis. Sweet! We picked up a couple of cucumbers for our wraps too. Fresh food is a treat if it holds up.

Then we came back here to freeze. Where I come from, if the temperature drops into the fifties, the heat is likely to come on, but not in Maine. Everywhere we went, the windows were open, and fans were blowing. Everywhere except the gas station store, which is air-conditioned, and so cold it was practically hostile to life. We're all packed up now. One more AYCE breakfast tomorrow, and we start the final run to Katahdin.

—

When I paid the bill at Shaw's I found out a lot of things I thought were free like laundry weren't. I made the mistake because there were no prices posted. They just said if I wanted to do laundry, here's the machine. No matter. It was a great place to stay, and the service was excellent.

It was raining when they drove us to the trail, and it rained on and off until late afternoon when it rained hard until after we got here. At lunchtime a hiker saw me putting cucumber slices in a wrap.

He said, "That isn't weight efficient".

I replied, "Maybe not, but it's morale efficient".

Sometime in the afternoon, the end fell off one of my Leki hiking poles. It's now held on by some duct tape that Vern gave me when I stayed at his place.

At the first ford of the day, we used our fording shoes, but by the time we got to the last and widest, our hiking shoes were soaked so we didn't bother. Big Wilson stream was maybe 75 feet across and the current was swift. I could tell Jan was uneasy about it so I told her to wait while I took my pack across, and came back. There was an overhead rope that I used to steady myself against the current. The bottom was very slippery, and when I was half way across, I slipped and went in up to my waist. I pulled myself erect, and went the rest of the way. I went back and got Jan. I put her pack on my back, showed her how to hook her arm over the rope if she thought she might lose her grip, and we forded without further incident. The Wilson Valley Lean-to is only seven tenths of a mile after the ford. We arrived having averaged one mile an hour. We're staying in the shelter because Jan was tired and setting up in here seemed like the path of least resistance. It's warmer than usual tonight. Maybe that will help me get through the night without feeling as if I've been beaten up.

—

We bought food for six days at 12 miles per day. We're not making it. We passed by Cloud Mountain Lean-to intending to make camp at 12 miles, but Jan said she was getting wobbly so we stopped in a spruce grove. Our plan now is to eat less but fortify our food with butter to keep the calories up. We're also hoping the trail conditions will improve. All we need is a few good miles to be caught up.

We had some interesting fords today. At one, I think it was Wilbur Brook, we had to reconnoiter when my pole went in up to the hilt. That was too deep with the current being as swift as it was.

It's cold and windy tonight. We made a big pot of mac and cheese, and had pie for desert. Lights out late tonight. 9 PM!

—

The trails were awful for most of today; innumerable steep rocky ups and downs, roots, and bogs. By lunchtime, we'd gone 4 miles, and Jan had banged her shin. It immediately started growing a big ugly goose egg. I applied a compression bandage and the swelling is suppressed so far.

I've been carrying Jan's pack, a cavernous 65 liter Deuter, for the last two days to help her keep up. Weight isn't much of a consideration for Jan. If she wants it, it goes in her pack. If she's afraid she'll forget her anvil at a campsite, she'll pack a spare. She's carrying my ultralight pack and minimalist gear now. She seems to be a little happier. The Deuter is mostly OK, but the adjustable mount for the shoulder belt harness presses on my back like a fist.

We finally got good, and then excellent trails, the kind that serve the general public, not just AT hikers after we passed Chairback Mountain late in the afternoon. We flew along after that. We were hiking through a popular day hiking area when we encountered a man at dusk who wasn't wearing pants. He quickly donned a pair of shorts, and as he passed us, he said he hadn't expected to meet anyone. We ran into four or five day hikers after that so I suspect that he had expected to meet someone, just not us.

Even with the good trails, we had to hike a couple of hours after dark to reach our mileage goal for the day and this site is rocky and boggy; not an issue if you hang in a hammock.

—

Today was better. Despite having to climb over four mountain peaks, we recovered two of the two point eight miles we'd gotten behind. Most of the trails were the kind you'd be happy to take your grandmother walking on. We even encountered numerous long rock staircases. The Maine Appalachian Trail Club has done a great job here. Coming off Whitecap, we got our first view of Katahdin. You can almost touch it with a long stick, but there are still 72 meandering trail miles before we get there. We made our miles and then some, and still got to East Branch Lean-to well before dark.

—

With only one hillock to summit and granny trails, we covered a lot of miles and still got to Antler Campground by 5:30. Antler is a beautiful public campground by a lake, and it's only six miles from Whitehouse Landing, our re-supply point to get us through the last fifty miles of the Hundred Mile Wilderness. It was a day of personal bests for

Jan. This is the furthest she's ever hiked, and the furthest she's ever hiked without re-supply.

Mount Katahdin, Jan and The Badger

—

Trails of mixed quality got us to Whitehouse Landing at 11 AM. Yesterday we met a man coming from here who warned us to blow the horn for boat pickup once and only once — the owner is widely reputed to be a curmudgeon — so we gave a short horn blast, and sat down on the dock to wait. We could make out activity in the yard at the landing as if the owner, Bill Ware, was daring us to blow the horn again, but after fifteen minutes, he motored over, and brought us to the lodge. When we got here:

Bill: Lunch or shower first?

me: Lunch.

Jan: Shower.

Therein lies the fundamental difference between men and women. A man figures, "I stink. I've been stinking for a week. What's another hour more or less? If I don't eat something, I'll die." A woman is thinking, "I'd rather be dead than smell like this for another instant". The weird thing is, they don't stink when they're thinking that. All I smell might be slight sweat odor, or maybe cedar or something. Anyway, I think we all know how it went after that.

We have a private room and access to a common room all of which is very clean. The shower is hot. The toilet is a pit privy, but very clean and well maintained. It doesn't stink, and they maintain a motion activated sanitizer dispenser right outside the door. Lunch and supper come with the lodging. I think breakfast is extra. I didn't see anything I liked on the main menu so I picked the one-pound cheeseburger from the hors d'oeuvres. We have free access to a canoe, and enjoy a nice yard with benches along the shore.

There is cellular telephone service, but strangely, they don't offer any sort of recharging. Power is scarce here. They generate their own via wind, solar, and LP gas, but phones and cameras are such a small draw, compared to say, their big screen TV that isn't on during the day that they could easily set something up. They seem clueless that it's little things like that that irritate people, especially someone using a cell phone to journal every night through 120 miles of wilderness, and wants to use a camera too.

Well, the place is for sale for, I've heard, $1.6 million. Beautiful as it is, I'm hard pressed to think of a business model that could make this place work at that price.

We re-supplied after supper. We're going to take it easy all the way to Katahdin so it will take us five days. We'll be stopping at all the vistas including a few side trips, and staying at every lean-to.

—

Well, I said we were going to take it easy, and we did. After a nice breakfast, we said goodbye to Whitehouse Landing. Linda Ware gave us a cucumber from her garden, which will add a little something to the lunch wraps for the next few days.

The trail was near water, rivers or lakes all day, and the weather was perfect. We came to a bridge at lunchtime, which was perfect because it took us to the sunny side of a river where we ate on a big rock.

Mid afternoon, we watered up from a spring flowing into Lake Nahmakanta, and rested on the sandy beach there for a while before hiking to Wadleigh Stream Lean-to around 3:30. We got the hammocks up, and went up to the Lean-to. We made a smoky fire to ward off the skeeters, and chatted with three other hikers, two of whom are going at more or less the same pace we are.

We ate a big pot of macaroni and cheese, and then we came back to the hammocks to rest up for tomorrow.

—

Our original plan was to do about eight miles to Rainbow Stream Lean-to, but we got there at two, and it started to rain. We figured we'd rather hike than sit in our hammocks in the rain all afternoon so we did another four miles.

Tomorrow we'll do ten miles to Abol Bridge where we'll enjoy a restaurant meal or two, and I'll supply for the next day's walk into Baxter State Park, and the climb up Mt. Katahdin to the Northern Terminus of the AT the day after that.

Jan and I will part company tomorrow for a couple of days. She had some difficulty on the steep climbs in the first half of the Hundred Mile Wilderness and wasn't sure she could keep up. I didn't like the idea of her turning back alone if she had to so we decided she'd go to Millinocket to make arrangements for the trip home.

There's several North bounders camping here tonight, and the word is that as many as thirty are converging on Abol to prepare for summiting on the 19th, the last sunny day before rain is predicted in Baxter. There's no air of excitement. Everyone is slowing down, and taking it easy. Some are planning a night of partying in Abol before the final two days.

—

The trails were as rocky and rooty as ever but the scent of the barn is a powerful motivator. This is a private campground and a de facto Katahdin staging area for hikers coming out of the Hundred Mile Wilderness. The atmosphere at Abol Bridge, quite literally in the shadow of Mount Katahdin, is festive. There are throngs of AT hikers milling about and the usual jugglers, wandering minstrels, dancing bears, hucksters, and fire-eaters.

Well, maybe not quite that festive, and what festivity there is, is mostly amongst the car campers who are oblivious of the AT hikers among them. I have fond childhood memories of car camping with my family, but it seems foreign, almost inane now.

Tomorrow, we'll walk a mile into the park, and register for a slot at the campsite near the base of the mountain nine miles farther down the trail. There's some talk that there are too many hikers for the space available. That would normally be a cause for concern given my hiking speed, but judging by the number of cases of beer I've seen headed for the hiker campsites, I have the feeling that a goodly number of them won't be registering before noon.

I plan to be up at the usual five AM. As a precaution, I purchased a half liter of chocolate milk from the campground store, which I can drink for breakfast on the trail.

Jan and I ate a leisurely lunch. We made sure everything I'd need was in my pack, and I put her on the shuttle to Millinocket at four thirty. I lounged around, and conversed with a few of the hikers camped nearby until suppertime. I sat down expecting to eat alone, but three hikers we met yesterday (a German couple, and a Peace Corps Veteran) invited me to their table, and we stuffed ourselves until we could stuff no more.

On the way back to my hang I ran into the four section hikers from Georgia that I first met at Pierce Pond Sporting Camps. They offered me a beer. I should have refused it, but how do you say no to free beer? I spent a few minutes with them. They all thought Jan was the world's best sport for not complaining despite the adversity she suffered in the wilderness. I was in pain by the time I made it back to my hammock. I had to lie down for half an hour and let digestion get to work before I could make my bed and climb into it. The weather is supposed to be good Monday.

I got up early because I had an uneasy feeling about registration. I hurried down to the kiosk and was the third person to sign the register for a slot at The Birches. The four from Georgia arrived about the same time. Then a girl from the party campsite showed up and filled out the remaining slots with names of her friends who were nowhere to be seen. This greatly upset a couple of hikers who came up a few minutes later while I was eating breakfast. They said to hell with it. They were going to show up at the ranger's office near camp and register. I imagined the ranger throwing up his hands in frustration, and registering the first twelve who showed up there.

With that in mind, I packed up my kitchen, and set out for The Birches at flank speed. I flew through the forest passing people who only days before had passed us in the wilderness like we were taking a nap. I was second to arrive at the ranger's office. He'd gotten word of what had happened at the kiosk, which was by now manned. He solved the problem by accepting everyone who showed up. So, having covered ten miles by ten thirty, I had a little time on my hands, as did quite a number of other hikers who filtered in for the rest of the morning.

The Georgia boys showed up as did their friend with a truck, two large pizzas, and ice cold Cokes which they gave to five of us sitting around the skeeter fire.

With so much time on their hands, the hikers did what comes naturally all afternoon; talked, cooked, and ate. Around three, I wandered off to bed for a nap. I got up around suppertime, cooked, ate, sat around the fire with the rest, and discoursed about this and that. A German fellow said it was boorish to wear shorts on a flight, which hit home because that was what I wore on my flight to New Hampshire last month. I wonder how he feels about skirts then. There's no real excitement in the air. The consensus is that there's one more hill to climb tomorrow before we all go home.

—

Last night's serenity may have been superficial. A day in camp usually begins in fits and starts amidst a chorus of coughs, farts, and scratching as one camper after another rises, and executes his personal ritual of cooking, packing, and leaving. The campsite waxes quiet and desolate, and remains so for some eight hours.

Today everyone was up at five and shortly thereafter was packed, and gone; everyone save me and the young couple I dined with at Abol. We took the time to eat a leisurely breakfast. Then it was off to the climb. There was nothing much special about it. I can lift my carcass at roughly twelve hundred feet per hour, and I did so today. I met the German person on his way down. He'd suffered an attack of vertigo in the alpine zone and had to turn back. Quite a letdown after hiking 2200 miles I'd say. I made the climb in three and a quarter hours, arriving at the summit at exactly sometime before noon in a wind that some said was gusting to 50 mph. From personal experience, I know a wind of that speed would knock me down, and it did not, but I think 30 mph would be a good estimate. It certainly was cause for concern on some of the steep rock climbs above the tree line.

There were probably twenty people at the summit when I arrived and the number stayed relatively constant as climbers came and went. Hugs were made, hands were shaken, and many pictures were taken. I hung around until the Georgia Four donned tuxedoes for the photograph that culminated their 16-year section hike. I got a few pics for myself before I descended. The descent was far more unnerving than the climb because facing down; I could see just how far I could fall.

When I reached the campground, I found an empty lean-to where I washed up and put on my town underpants. Then I hitched a ride to Millinocket and met up with Jan. I weighed myself at the Lodge. I was down 12 pounds. Sweet! There was major gorging in my immediate future.

We had a big restaurant meal, but I wasn't up to the final challenge; that of eating a giant ice cream sundae that is free if you finish it. I did the traditional signing of a ceiling panel in the restaurant, noting the signatures of DreamTime and others I'd met last year. Then we came back here to the inn to get some much-needed sleep.

Tomorrow we'll journey to Virginia, there to live out our days in the comfort, and security of our beloved Badger Hall.

Epilogue

It's been a few years since my long hike. I've made two runs at The Pacific Crest Trail since then; once with DreamTime and once alone. Both were ended by injury at about four hundred miles. I'm happy to say that DreamTime persevered without me and completed her hike. I've done numerous shorter backpacking trips. That's probably my future.

This year I started volunteering as a trail steward for The Potomac Area Trails Club. It's given me a deep appreciation for the tremendous amount of work that goes into keeping the trails passable and safe. If anything I've written about trail maintainers is unkind, I take it back, and promise never again.

I'm glad that I faithfully kept this journal. As superficial and incomplete as it is, it enlivens my memories whenever I read from it. I'm grateful for that, but it came at a price. While the others in the camps and shelters slumbered or socialized, I was in my hammock, hunched over a miniature keyboard virtually every single night. Judging by what I didn't miss out on, I missed out on a lot.

I'm amazed that I hung on so long the first year. Maybe it was because the deterioration was so gradual that I didn't notice it; like the frog that dies in a gradually heated pot of water. It took a debilitating injury to wake me up. What a difference a year off makes!

There were good times and bad, triumphs and defeats. The best times were those I enjoyed with family, friends, and fellow hikers. My nadir was the descent to Garfield Shelter in a deluge of singular magnitude. I felt isolated and alone, but any loneliness or disappointments I may have felt along the way pale before the adventure of a lifetime.

Index

3

3C's Restaurant, 119

A

Abol Bridge, 209, 210
Africa, 82
Albert Mountain, 13
Amicalola Falls, *1*, 3, 10
Andover, 180, 188, 189
Andy. *See* Hamm, Padla, Sink
Antler Campground, 206
Appalachian Moujntain Club,
   168
Appalachian Trail Conservancy,
   103, 106
Applesauce, 43
Asolo, 79
AT Museum, 111
Atkins, 63
Avatar, 29, 31, 35, 37
Avery Memorial Campsite, 198
AwesomePossum, 56
AZCruiser, 162

B

BabySteps, 20, 61
Backcountry, 72
Balchik, Nancy, 78
Bald Mountain, 40
Bald Pate, 187, 188
Balls and Sunshine, 96
Bascom Lodge, 151
Beagle Boys, 11
Beahms Gap Overlook, 96
Bear Mountain, 132, 143, 156
Beaver Creek, 57
Bemis Peaks, 189
Ben, 190
Bennington, 149, 152
Big Meadow, 93, 94, 95
Big Walker Hotel, 65

Bigelow Peaks, 198
Bill Ackerly, 162
Billy, 122
Black Mountain, 131
Blacksburg, 72
blind hiker, 193
BlisterQueen, 135
Blood Mountain, 5
Boiling Springs, 113
BoJangles, 178
Bolder, 2, 7, 8, 9, 10, 11, 12, 13,
   14, 22
Boy Scout, 101, 154
Bradley Gap, 48
Breezy Inn, 129
Brennan, Pat, 26
BronzeBeard, *1*
Brushy Mountain, 63
Budget Inn
   Franklin, 14
   Hiawassee, 9
Buena Vista, 83
Buladean, 46

C

Cabin
   Upper Goose Pond, 146
Cable Gap, 22
CandyMan, 36, 100, 110
Caratunk, 199, 200
Carver's Gap, 48
Catawba, 66, 72
Charleston, 20
cheese factory, 8
Cherokee, 25, 26
Cheshire, 150
Clingmans Dome, 25
Connie, 46
Corbie, 155
Corner Grill, 43
CrankDaddy, 39, 40, 41
Crawford Gap, 166, 171, 173
Crawford Notch, 177

217

Crocker Cirque Campsite, 195
Crocker Mountain, 195

D

Dahlgren Campground, 104
Dairy King, 57
Dairy Queen, 70
Daleville, 76, 79
Dalton, 148, 149
Damascus, 51, 54, 55, 56, 58
Daniel, 128, 129, 131, 132, 133
Dartmouth Outdoor Club, 164
Dave, 15
Delaware River Bridge, 125
Delaware Water Gap, 123
Dick's Creek Gap, 9
Dicks Dome Shelter, 100
DigIt. *See* Diva
Diva, 8, 9, 22, 53
Dollar General, 52, 58
Donu, *1*, 2, 3, 4, 6, 8, 9, 10, 11,
    16, 19, 24, 25, 29, 31, 153
Dora, 115
DOS, 21, 149
Doyle, 113, 114, 116, 118
DragonFly, 191
DreamTime, 138, 139, 143, 180,
    181, 182, 183, 185, 187, 189,
    190, 191, 214, 215
Duffer, 120, 122, 123, 124, 125,
    128, 129, 130, 134, 146
Duncannon, 109, 113

E

EagleEye, 59, 66, 68, 69, 70, 71
East Flagstaff Lake, 198
Econo-lodge, 62
Edward R. Morrow Memorial
    Park, 136
Elk Gardens, 59
Elke, 71
Elkton, 92
Elkwallow Wayside, 96
Emilie, 9, 72

Emily, 2
Erwin, 35, 37, 41, 43, 45, 49, 53
Expediter, 52, 91

F

Fayetteville, 108, 109
FivePair, 148
Flamingo Restaurant, 109, 110
Flash, 155, 198
Flint Mountain Shelter, 37
Florida, 11, 48
Floyd Mountain, 80
Fontana, 20, 21, 36, 53
Fontana lodge, 22
Food Lion, 26, 84, 92
Four State Challenge, 106
Franklin, 8, 11, 13, 15, 156
Fresh, 115
Front Royal, 96, 100
FruitLoop, 93
Funk, 178

G

Gale River, 173
Gatlinburg, 25, 29, 31
Georgia Four, 214
Giamatti, Paul, 16
GoodDeeds, 56, 58, 63
Gorham, 175, 181, 183, 185
Gorp, 92, 104
GourmetGirls, 68, 69, 70, 82, 146
Grayson Highlands, 60
Greasy Cove, 44
Great Smokey Mountains
    National Park, 23, 27, 28, 31,
    71
Green Mountains, 160
Greenville, 203
Greenwood Lake, 128, 130

H

Half-Gallon Challenge, 68, 111,
    115

Hamm, Andy, 9, 110, 114, 115, 116
Hampton, 51
Hanover, 159, 160
Harper's Ferry, 62, 103, 104
Haven, Ron, 14
Height of Land, 191
Heinrich, 7, 64, 69, 70, 71, 72, 81, 117, 175, 178, 179, 180, 184
HemlockMuppet, 59
Hennessy Hyper-light Backpacker, 77
Hiawassee, 8, 9, 15
High Rock, 107
Highpoint State Park, 126
Hike Naked Day, 129
Hogback, 37, 40
HoJo's, 78
Hoot, 80, 81, 82, 83, 130
Hostel
    4 Pines, 75, 77, 81
    Bear's Den, 102
    Glencliff Hiker's Welcome, 164
    Greasy Creek, 45, 46
    Green Mountain, 157
    Hiker, 1, 67, 158
    Kinkora, 49
    Laughing Heart, 32, 33
    Maria McCabe's, 139
    Mountain Harbor, 49
    Mountain House, 154
    Shaw's, 202, 203
    Standing Bear Farm, 29, 46
    Uncle Johnny's, 41, 44, 45, 46, 145
    White Mountains, 183
    Whitehouse Landing, 206, 207, 209
    Wood's Hole, 67
Hot Springs, 30, 31, 32, 34, 36, 49, 56, 78, 196
Hotsauce, 65
Housatonic River, 138

Hudson River, 125, 128, 129, 131, 133
Humpback Mountain, 48
Hundred Mile Wilderness, 206, 210
Huntsville, 37
Hut
    Bearfence, 93
    Blackrock, 90
    Carter, 181
    Galehead, 173, 175, 186
    Hight Top, 93
    Lakes of the Clouds, 178
    Mizpah, 178
    Pinefield, 91
    Rock Springs, 95
    Zealand, 176, 177

I

Illinois Outlaws, 22
Imp Camp, 181
Ingles, 15
Instigator, 52, 91
Iron Furnace State Park, 111
Irwin, 44
Island Pond, 131

J

Jack, 67, 71
James Madison U, 93
James River, 82
Jan, 9, 19, 26, 32, 33, 42, 51, 63, 70, 87, 89, 91, 92, 93, 95, 97, 98, 100, 101, 103, 107, 108, 136, 172, 173, 177, 200, 201, 202, 203, 204, 205, 207, 210, 211, 214
Jane, 7
Janet, 39
JBone, 19, 20
Jeri and Greg, 183
JerseyBoys, 28, 32, 133, 149
Joe, 12, 75, 76
Joe Dodge Lodge, 175, 179

219

Joe's Carpentry, 12
Johannes, 73
Jones Falls, 50
Josh, *1*
Julia, 20

K

Kaltsos, Angelo, 189
Katahdin, 133, 189, 199, 203,
   206, 209, 210
Kazakhstan, 103
Keffer Oak, 73
Kelly
   Pat, 114
   Vicky, 114
Kenebec River, 199, 200
Kinsman Mountain, 166, 167
KitFox, 111, 165
Knot Maul, 63
Kroger, 72, 78, 80, 89

L

Lake Nahmakanta, 209
Lake Watauga, 52
Lakota Lake Lookout, 159
Laurel Falls, 50
Lean-to
   Bemis, 190
   Cloud Mountain, 205
   East Branch, 206
   Horseshoe Canyon, 201
   Rainbow Stream, 209
   Spaulding Mountain, 193
   Wadleigh Stream, 209
   Wilson Valley, 204
Lemon Squeezer, 131
Lewis and Clark, 82
Lewis Mountain Campground, 93
Little Saddleback Mountain, 192
Loft Mountain Store, 88
Loft Mountain Wayside, 91, 92
Long Pond, 130
Lorax, 156

M

MacheteMitch, 17, 49
MacKaye, Benton, 153
Magpie, 153
Mahoosuc Arm, 186
Mahoosuc Notch, 184, 185, 186
Maine, 50, 153, 159, 160, 184,
   203, 206
Maine Appalachian Trail Club,
   201
Maine Junction, 159
MakeTime, 34, 42, 43, 44, 53,
   AKA MakeTime2
MamawB, 134, 135, 136, 160,
   168
Manchester, 153, 154, 157
ManCub, 111, 165
Maniac, 120
Maryland Challenge, 68
Massachusetts, 141, 150, 151
Max Patch, 31
Mayberry, 42
McAffee Knob, 76
McCabe, Maria, 139, 141
McDonald's, 52, 78, 92, 116,
   183, 187
MellowYellow, 63
Memorial Day, 101
Microtel, 25, 26
MidwesternMamma, 181, 184,
   185
Mike, 99
MilesToGo, 198
Millinocket, 210, 211, *214*
Mo, 24
Moe's, 3
Monson, 200, 201, 202, 203
Mother and Son, 17, 19, 22, 50
Mount Bushnell, 144
Mount Cube, 163
Mount Everett, 143
Mount Greylock, 150, 151
Mount LaFayette, 172, 173
Mount Mousilauke, 165, 167
Mount Rogers Outfitters, 57

Mount Washington, 104, 178, 179
Mountain Crossing, 5
Mountford, Robert, 67
Mouse, 115
Moxie Bald, 200
MrBurns, 167
MrWrong, 102, 107, 122
Muldoon, 8
Murray Property, 127, 128

N

Natahala Outdoor Center, 17, 18, 19
Natahala River, 18
Nelson, Jody, 35
Nelson, John, 35
New Found Gap, 25, 26, 27
New Hampshire, 159, 160, 170
New Jersey, 122, 123, 125, 127
Newfound Gap, 25
NOC. *See* Natahala Outdoor Center
NoHear'Em, 90, 91
NoodleHeads, 143, 147
North Adams, 151
North Carolina, 9
NutterButter, 136

O

Obamacare, 137
Ohleger, Michael, 84
Old Blue Mountain, 189
Old Speck Mountain, 187
OldGoose, 138, 139, 143
Ore Hill Camp, 163
Osgood Trail, 179
Outhouse Chronicles,The, 189
Overmountain Shelter, 48

P

Pacific Crest Trail, 215
Padla

Andy, 139, 142, 180, 181, 182, 183, 188, 189
PaintedLady, 181, 184
Pater, 9
Pawling, 135, 136
Peace Corps, 103, 115, 211
Pearisburg, 64, 65, 69, 71, 82
Pen Mar Park, 105, 107
Pennsylvania, 116, 118, 125
PeppaBoy, 163
Pierce Pond Sporting Camps, 203, 211
Pinnacle Picnic Area, 96
Pittsfield, 147
Plaza Motel, 70
Pocono Inn, 123
Port Clinton Hotel, 118
Potomac Area Trails Club, 102, 107, 215
PrincessDoah, 168

R

Rainbow, 136, 168
Ramsay, Laura Susan, 67
Rangely, 190, 191
Rattlesnake Spring Campground, 125
Raven Rocks Shelter, 105
Reddington Camp, 191
Rentschler Marker, 118
Resource, 69, 82
Ricky Wilson, 44
Ricky Wilson's Barber Shop, 42
Roan Mountain, 47, 59
Roanoke Trails Club, 75
Rockfish Gap, 87, 93
Rocksylvania, 123
Rocky Top Tennessee, 24
Rutland, 158, 159

S

Salisbury, 139
SaltBomb, 50, 63, 64, 68, 69
Sarge, 42, 44

Schaghticoke Connecticut
  Campsite, 138
Schneckelholfer, 126, 128
ScrewLoose, 23, 29, 31, 32, 45,
  46, 48, 49, 51
Seinfeld, 14
Sharon, 141, 142
Shelter
  Bake Oven Knob, 121
  Bald Mountain, 40
  Bobblet's Gap, 79
  Bryant Ridge, 80
  Carter Gap, 11
  Chatfield, 63
  Cold Spring, 17
  Congdon, 152
  Copper Lodge, 158
  Cosby Knob, 28
  Darlington, 113
  David Lesser, 102
  Derrick Knob, 25
  Ed Garvey, 103
  Eliza Brook, 166
  Elkville, 119
  Ensign Cowell, 105
  Fontana Hilton, 21
  Garfield, 172, 216
  Gooch Mountain, 3
  Gren Anderson, 126, 127
  Harper's Creek, 85
  Hawk Mountain, 2
  Hogback Ridge, 37
  Hurricane Mountain, 61
  Iceberg Springs, 27
  Iron Mountain, 53
  Jenkins, 64
  Jenny Knob, 67
  Jerry Cabin, 37
  Kid Gore, 153
  Kinkora, 51
  Lambert's Meadow, 77
  Laurel Fork, 50
  Lost Mountain, 59, 60
  Lost Pond, 155
  Low Gap, 6
  Matt's Creek, 82
  Maupin Field, 85
  Minerva Hinchey, 156
  Mollies Ridge, 23
  Moose Mountain, 162
  Morgan Stewart, 135
  Mount Wilcox North, 145
  Muskrat Creek, 10
  Niday, 73
  No Business Knob, 41
  Overmountain, 49
  Partnership, 61, 62
  Paul C. Wolfe, 87
  Peck's Corner, 27
  Pete's Mountain, 114
  Pine Knob, 104
  Pine Swamp Branch, 71
  Punchbowl, 82, 83
  Raven Rocks, 107
  Rock Gap, 13
  Sam Moore, 101
  Sassafras Gap, 19, 20
  Saunders, 59
  Seely Woodworth, 85
  Speck Pond, 187
  Tagg Run, 112
  The Priest, 85
  Tom Floyd Wayside, 97
  Tom's Run, 110
  Tray Mountain, 8
  Tumbling Run, 108
  Vandeventer, 52, 54
  Wapiti, 67
  Warspur, 71
  Watauga Lake, 52
  Wayah Bald, 15, 16
  Wesser Bald, 17
  Wise, 61
Shenandoah National Park, 88,
  97
Shenandoah Valley, 86, 93
Sink, Andy, 147, 148
SitABit, 106, 107, 175, 179
Skyline Drive, 91, 92, 95, 97
Smiley, 23, 29, 31, 49
Snowbird Mountain, 30
Snuffy Smith, 13

222

Spider, 145
Springer Mountain, *1*
Stanton. *See* Staunton
Stats, 94, 156
Staunton, 88, 99
Steve, 137
Steven Breyer, 52
Stoke's Steakhouse, 126
Stratton, 153, 195, 196, 197, 198
Stratton Mountain, 153
StrayDog, 77, 79, 80, 93
Street Gap, 39
Styles Peak, 155
Sunshine. *See* Balls and Sunshine
SweetTea, 106, 107
Swinging Lick Gap, 15

T

T, 148
Tennessee, 36, 99, 145
Tennessee Valley Authority, 21
TenYear, 126, 127, 128, 135
Teresa's Diner, 51
Tesnatee Gap, 6
The Birches, 212
The Roller Coaster, 101, 102
The Sage of Hot Springs, 49, 67
Three Amigos, 176
TickleMonster, 45, 47
Tim, 199
Tinker Cliffs, 77
Tom Levardi, 149
trail magic, 8
TrailMix, 37, 73, 92
Trog, 138, 139, 143
Tuchi, 19, 20
Turtle and Taken. *See* Mother
    and Son
Tye River, 85

U

Uncorked, 84

Unionville, 128
Uno, 8, 9, 12, 53

V

Vermont, 150, 152, 156, 158, 160
Vern, 187, 188, 189, 190, 204
Virginia, 26, 47, 56, 86, 99, 104,
    130, 171, 178, 214
Virginia Creeper Trail, 57

W

WalkSoftly, 28, 34, 42, 43, 44,
    53
WallStreet, 101
Wal-Mart, 52, 69, 107, 119, 136,
    158, 183
Ware
    Bill, 207
    Linda, 209
Watauga Lake, 120
Waynesboro, 44, 87, 89, 93, 146
West Virginia, 100, 104
Wheeling, 20
White Mountains, 129
Whiterock Cliff, 36
Whitewater, 69
Whoop, 69, 82
Wilbur Brook, 205
Wind Gap, 122, 123
Wonder, 115, 126
Woody Gap, 3, 4
WornHeel, 183, 197

Y

Yellow Delli, 159
Yonder, 39

Z

ZZTopless, 201

AUG – 5 2021

9 781976 977367